The Brussels Encounter

OHRA

William Hartston
Willi Iclicki
Roger Lancaster

Annotations by:

Garry Kasparov

Lajos Portisch

John Nunn

Raymond Keene

Andrew Martin

BBC
Chess Classic

A CHEQUERS CHESS PUBLICATION

© Chequers Chess Publications 1987
18 Chalk Farm Road, London NW1.

First Edition 1987

ISBN 1-870207-40-8 (Limp)
ISBN 1-870207-35-1 (Hardback)

Printed in Great Britain by
Underhill (Plymouth) Limited, Plymouth.

FOREWORD and acknowledgments

The OHRA tournament, played in Brussels in December 1986, was a chess event of exceptionally high calibre. Indeed, in terms of the average Elo ratings of the contestants it was the strongest tournament in the history of the game. In addition, it was the first tournament in which Kasparov had competed for three years, his first as world champion.

For these reasons, the BBC chose OHRA Brussels for its new Chess Classic series. Using the 'voice-over' techniques made popular by the old Master Game programmes, viewers are given an opportunity to eavesdrop on the grandmasters' thoughts. We are indebted to the BBC for permission to reproduce extracts from these players' thought tracks in this volume. We should also like to thank Chess Classics Producer, Wendy Sturgess, for her encouragement in bringing this book out quickly, to coincide with transmission of the series.

Thirteen games were covered by the BBC. This book includes those games as well as the other seventeen played in the tournament. Every game is annotated, as follows:

Raymond Keene: Games 1, 3, 4, 5, 11, 12, 13, 14, 16, 17, 18, 20, 24, 26, 27, 28, 29, 30.
Andrew Martin: 2, 5, 7, 8, 21, 24, 25
Lajos Portisch: 6, 8, 21, 23.
Garry Kasparov: 10, 25.
John Nunn: 21.

The story behind the OHRA tournament

From the very start, I had three objectives:

1. To find a great sponsor;
2. To ensure the participation of the world champion;
3. To make sure that the tournament had some exceptional dimension.

Already in 1985, OHRA, a Dutch insurance company also established in Belgium, had sponsored a grandmaster tournament. When approached for an event in 1986, they were happy to agree to the suggested budget. As co-sponsors, the Hyatt Regency Hotel provided the necessary facilities for the players and organisers.

Next on the list came the world champion, whom I met in London before his match with Karpov. Kasparov indicated that he would be happy to play, as long as he retained his title, and provided the tournament was at least of FIDE Category 15.

Once Kasparov's pariticpation was assured, the rest followed easily - publicity for the event came easily, and the world's strongest players indicated their interest to compete against the champion.

We invited **Viktor Korchnoi**, winner of the 1985 OHRA tournament, whose Elo rating of 2650 ranked him third in the world. Then we chose **Robert Hübner**, 2625, in joint fourth place in the world. **Nigel Short**, at 21 years old, was already rated top in England and ninth in the world at 2615. **Lajos Portisch**, 2605, for so long a leading contender for the world title. Finally came **John Nunn**, at 2595 second in Britain and threatening to break through the 2600 barrier.

Willi Iclicki
Tournament organiser

CONTENTS

TOURNOI INTERNATIONAL D'ECHECS OHRA
DU 12 AU 23 DECEMBRE 1986 DE 13 à 19 H

INTERNATIONAAL OHRA SCHAAK TORNOOI
VAN 12 TOT EN MET 23 DECEMBER 1986 VAN 13 TOT 19 U

HYATT REGENCY BRUSSELS – RUE ROYALE 250 KONINGSSTRAAT – BRUXELLES/BRUSSEL

ROUND ONE:

Portisch	½:½	Short
Nunn	0:1	Kasparov
Korchnoi	1:0	Hübner

Far too often in tournaments of the highest class, many of the games end in quick draws. The combative spirit at OHRA, however, was excellent and the first round was typical of what was to follow. Perhaps the players appetites had been sharpened by a long and inconclusive argument about playing schedules the previous evening. Whatever the reason, only Portisch and Short showed normal first round caution. Nunn's opening experiment, the unusual 8 ♕d3, was dealt with harshly by the world champion. Hübner was the unlucky man of the day, blundering on move 36 when in a better position.

OFF THE BOARD

Chess tournaments, even grandmaster tournaments, do not have a reputation for being organised with military precision.

Although a daily one o'clock start had been pre-agreed, some of the grandmasters decided on arrival that three o'clock would be more congenial.

Protracted negotiations between the players, led by Kasparov, and the organisers followed with compromise factions on both sides prepared to settle for two o'clock instead.

"If we take so long over agreeing such small things, how shall we ever agree over serious matters such as the Grand Prix money", lamented Lajos Portisch, whereupon everyone settled on three o'clock. Latest rumour was a US$2,000,000 Grand Prix prize fund.

The opening ceremony was therefore late but all then went well until the time came for the players to be publicly introduced, which was due to happen in descending order of ELO seniority.

The OHRA managing director successfully negotiated Kasparov, Korchnoi and Hübner but then omitted Short and moved straight on to Portisch. An immobile Portisch gesticulated at Short to move forward.

Unfortunately, Short was facing the opposite direction so Portisch's gestures were completely lost on him. However, with the aid of a certain amount of nudging and pushing, the young Englishman was introduced to the audience followed in turn by Portisch and Nunn.

The organisers breathed sighs of relief. Running a tournament is child's play compared with ensuring that opening and closing ceremonies are marred by nothing more serious than the odd minor hitch.

GAME ONE

PORTISCH - SHORT

1 d4 e6 2 c4 ♘f6 3 ♘f3 d5 4 ♘c3 ♗e7 5 ♗g5
0-0 6 e3 h6 7 ♗xf6 ♗xf6 8 ♖c1 a6 9 a3 c6 10
♗d3 ♘d7 11 0-0 b5 12 cxb5 cxb5 13 ♗b1
♗b7 14 a4 bxa4 15 ♘xa4 ♖c8 16 ♕d3 g6 17
b4 ♗c6 18 ♕b3 ♗xa4 19 ♕xa4 ♘b8 20 ♗d3
½:½

GAME ONE

PORTISCH · SHORT

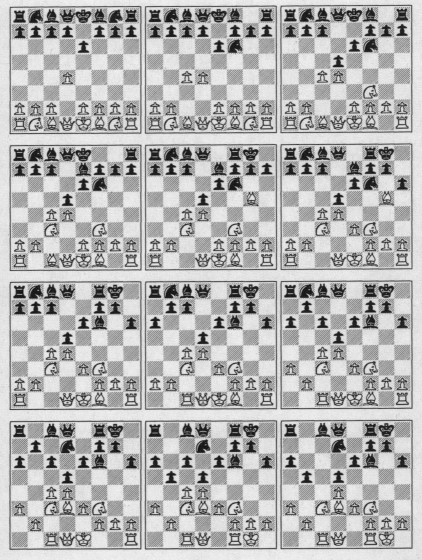

½:½

11

Portisch - Short

1	d4	e6
2	c4	

Declining the invitation (via 2 e4) to a French, one of Nigel's first loves.

2	...	♘f6
3	♘f3	d5
4	♘c3	♗e7
5	♗g5	0-0
6	e3	h6
7	♗xf6	

Kasparov's favourite.

7	...	♗xf6
8	♖c1	a6!?

Short equalises easily enough with this bizarre move against Portisch, one of the greatest exponents of 1 d4. Significantly though, Nigel did not repeat this innovation when he faced Kasparov later in the tournament.

9	a3

The famous 'fight for tempo'. Portisch does not want to develop his King's Bishop and lose a tempo to ... dxc4. He also hopes eventually to drop his KB back to a2 when it does reach c4. However, Short has a quite different idea in mind from ... dxc4. 9 ♕c2 seems more to the point than Portisch's a3.

9	...	c6
10	♗d3	

Now 10 ... dxc4 11 ♗xc4 b5 12 ♗a2 would favour White.

10	...	♘d7
11	0-0	

11 c5 e5! does not promise White much.

11	...	b5!

An excellent equalising idea. Portisch had probably been expecting 11 ... dxc4 12 ♗xc4 e5.

12	cxb5	cxb5
13	♗b1	

13 e4 dxe4 14 ♘xe4 ♗b7 15 ♘d6 ♗d5 is fine for Black, as is 13 a4 b4 14 ♘b1 ♕b6 15 ♘bd2 ♗b7.

13	...	♗b7
14	a4	bxa4

Now that White has withdrawn his Bishop to b1 this is

a good alternative to ... b4.

15 ♘xa4 ♖c8
16 ♕d3 g6
17 b4 ♗c6
18 ♕b3

White only invites problems for himself with 18 ♕xa6? ♘b8!

18 ... ♗xa4

A practical decision, giving up the nebulous advantage of the Bishop pair in order to neutralise any shred of White advantage on the Q-file.

19 ♕xa4 ♘b8
20 ♗d3

Drawn.

That is the way Capablanca and Karpov could easily draw the teeth of strong opponents playing White. Short's 8 ... a6!? needs further testing as a possibly viable antidote to Kasparov's favourite line.

Nigel Short faced with a familiar position.

13

GAME TWO
NUNN-KASPAROV

1 e4 c5 2 ♘f3 d6 3 d4 cd 4 ♘xd4 ♘f6 5 ♘c3
a6 6 ♗g5 e6 7 f4 ♛b6 8 ♛d3 ♛xb2 9 ♖b1
♛a3 10 f5 ♗e7 11 ♗e2 ♘c6 12 fe fe 13 ♘xc6
bc 14 e5 de 15 ♗xf6 gf 16 ♗h5+ ♚f8 17
♛d2 ♚g7 18 ♖b3 ♛a5 19 0-0 ♖g8 20 ♚h1
♚h8 21 ♛h6 ♛d8 22 ♘e4 f5 23 ♗f7 ♛f8 24
♛h5 ♖g7 25 ♗e8 a5 26 ♗xc6 ♗a6 27 ♖f2
♖d8 0:1

GAME TWO

NUNN — KASPAROV

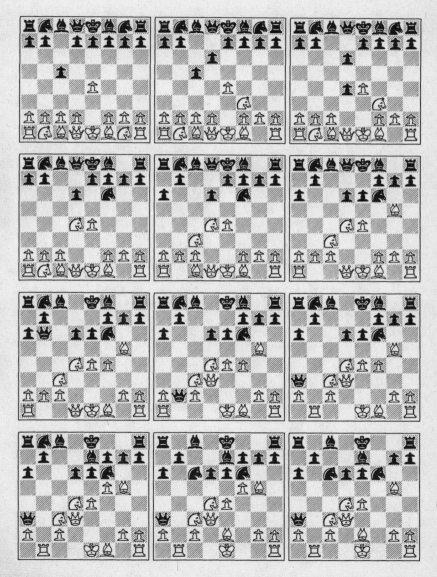

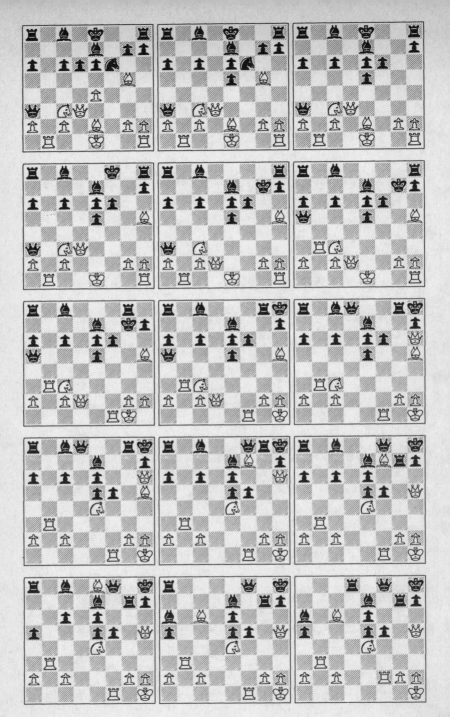

Nunn - Kasparov

1	e4	c5
2	♘f3	d6
3	d4	cxd4
4	♘xd4	♘f6
5	♘c3	a6
6	♗g5	

Nunn appears ready for a theoretical duel. Against Kasparov this is a very dangerous game to play.

6	...	e6
7	f4	♛b6
8	♛d3!?	

Usual is 8 ♛d2

8	...	♛xb2
9	♖b1	♛a3
10	f5	♗e7!

After 10 ... ♛a5!? 11 ♛c4 ♛d8 12 ♗d2 ♛c5 Jadoul-Nunn Brussels 1985, Nunn gives 13 fxe6! b5 14 ♛d3 fxe6 15 a4! with a winning position for White.

Why not 10 ... ♘c6? Black then has a choice after 11 fxe6 fxe6 12 ♘xc6 bxc6 13 e5 dxe5 14 ♗xf6 gxf6 15 ♗e2 of:

a) 15 ... ♗e7 Van der Wiel-Gavrikov London 1985 and;

b) 15 ... ♗c5 16 ♗h5+ ♔e7 17 ♛g3 ♖g8! (but not 17 ... ♗d7 18 ♛g7+ ♔d6 19 ♖d1+ ♗d4 20 ♖xd4+! exd4 21 ♛g3+ ♔c5 22 ♘e4+ ♔b4 23 c3! +1 Nunn) 18 ♛xg8 ♛xc3+ with perpetual check.

I think that the advantage of 10 ... ♗e7 is that it allows Kasparov to favourably transpose to Van der Wiel-Gavrikov without allowing the possibility of 14 ♖b3! ♛d6 (14 ... ♛a5 15 ♗xf6 gxf6 16 ♛f3) 15 ♛f3! with the idea of ♗xf6 and ♘e4.

Such long and complicated analysis is typical of the Poisoned Pawn. One slight mistake by either side is often enough to decide the game.

11	♗e2	

After 11 fxe6 (11 ♛c4 0-0) fxe6 12 ♛c4 0-0! 13 ♖b3 ♛c5 14 ♘xe6 ♗xe6 15 ♛xe6+ ♔h8 16 ♛xe7 ♘c6 it's the White King that is in greater danger.

11	...	♘c6
12	fxe6	fxe6
13	♘xc6	bxc6
14	e5	

17

14 0-0 is met by ♕c5+ and 14 ♘h5+ is repelled by 14 ... ♘xh5 15 ♗xe7 ♘f4! 16 ♕g3 e5.

14 ...   dxe5
15 ♗xf6   gxf6

The Black King hides under a sturdy screen of pawns and Bishops. 15 ... ♗xf6 is dangerous, eg. 16 ♗h5+ g6 17 ♗xg6+

16 ♗h5+   ♔f8
17 ♕d2?

We're still following the Van der Wiel game mentioned earlier but here Nunn deviates from the 17 0-0 e4! 18 ♕h3 f5 19 ♔h1 ♖g8 20 ♖b3 ♕c5 21 ♘e4 ♕xc2 where Black had an advantage.

17 ♕d2 threatens 18 ♕h6+ but as this is easily frustrated White may have to try 17 ♖f1!? if he wants anything; eg. 17 ♖f1 ♖f8 18 ♖f3 ♔g7 19 ♖h3 ♕d6 20 ♕f3 f5 21 ♗f7! But perhaps this position is fully defensible for Black anyway.

17 ...   ♔g7!
Kasparov aims to safety his King with ... ♖g8 and ♔h8 and then win with his extra pawn. White must do something quick.

18 ♖b3
18 ♘e4 ♖d8!
18 ...   ♕a5
18 ... ♕c5 19 ♘e4
19 0-0   ♖g8
20 ♔h1   ♔h8

Black is crouching, ready to hit back. It's difficult for White to attack any more.

21 ♕h6   ♕d8
22 ♘e4   f5!
23 ♗f7
23 ♖d3 ♗g5!
23 ...   ♕f8
24 ♕h5   ♖g7
White has shot his bolt. Nunn tries to hustle a mistake out of Kasparov with a Bishop lurch, but Black calmly co-ordinates and that is that.

25 ♗e8   a5!
Preparing ♗c8-a6
26 ♗xc6   ♗a6!

27 ♖f2 ♖d8

0:1

Not at all premature. White's a pawn down and he doesn't have any good moves. Against the World Champion that is quite enough.

Martin — Gutman

OFF THE BOARD

Naturally, world champion Gary Kasparov was the centre of media attention when he arrived in Brussels with scarcely a break from competing in the Olympiad at Dubai.

Nunn, Portisch and Short had also played there but Kasparov, in particular, felt fatigued. He attributed this partly to the chess games and partly to a political dimension for, once his game had finished, Kasparov often found himself negotiating a particular objective in a quite Dubai hotel room.

It said something for the champion's stamina that his score of 8½/11 was calculated, at ELO 2753, the most meritorious at Dubai.

The world champion nevertheless expressed the hope that he would win the Brussels event and, sure enough, time was to prove that he would do so with a two-point margin.

It was also remarked upon that, instead of being accompanied by Gurevich as expected, Kasparov was seconded by the older master, Nikitin.

Andrew Page, Kasparov's business manager, later explained that Gary's mother had suggested that, in Belgium, the young world champion might benefit through having at hand someone who was more of a father figure.

— The Players TV commentaries

1	e4	c5
2	♘f3	d6
3	d4	cd
4	♘xd4	♘f6
5	♘c3	a6
6	♗g5	

KASPAROV: This is the first time in my praxis to play against ♗g5. Of course I have prepared it carefully, but Karpov always played ♗e2 and quiet positions in Scheveningen variations. Now I have my first chance to show my preparation in the sharpest line of the Najdorf variation.

6	...	e6
7	f4	

KASPAROV: ♕b6 is the most principled line. Of course I have analysed other lines in this variation, but this is, in my opinion, the most principled. I am a little worried because I know that John is big specialist in this line.

7	...	♕b6

NUNN: This is a rather unpleasant surprise for me. I play this variation myself with Black and over the years I've been trying to convince myself that it really is good for Black and now I've got to try and convince myself it's good for White. I could, of course, play the main line here; with ♕d2 we play 20 moves of theory, then we play five moves of chess and the game's over. But perhaps I can give him a little surprise myself. It's the unusual move ♕d3, which has been played by the Dutch grandmaster van der Wiel with some success. Yes, let's go out on relatively unexplored paths.

8	♕d3	♕xb2
9	♖b1	♕a3

NUNN: In this position we must both be thinking about what differences it makes having the queen on d3 rather than d2. In some ways the queen's better on d3 — it can swing over to the king-side to g3. Perhaps in some lines it can even go to c4, but on the other hand the knight on c3 is difficult to move because I'm a pawn down and cannot allow exchange of queens. The move I think probably is best is to play just as if the queen were on d2 and to play f5.

10	f5	

KASPAROV: I suspect that I know this position much better than John could have expected. I remember a game when John played ♕a5 here. It's a bad move — after ♕c4 Black's position is very dangerous, maybe losing. Gavrikov played ♘c6 against van der Wiel. Maybe it's the best in this position. But in my opinion there is another move, ♗e7. The idea is to play after 11 ♕c4, 0-0 and it's impossible to take on e6 because 12 fxe6 fxe6 13 ♘xe6 and then b5. That is the idea.

10 ...   ♗e7
11 ♗e2   ♘c6

NUNN: Yes, that's a very natural move. He wants to exchange my knight or possibly put his knight on e5, so I've really got to do something forcing immediately here to try and make use of my lead in development. Quite often one exchanges on e6 then on c6 in such positions. I wonder if here that leads to a strong attack or whether it just leads to nothing. But in fact I think I'm already committed, I can't see any other way to continue the attack other than to make this series of exchanges.

12 fxe6   fxe6
13 ♘xc6   bxc6

NUNN: I'd really like to play ♗h5+ in this position but I see now something I didn't notice a couple of moves ago.

Black can play 14 ... ♘xh5 and after 15 ♗xe7 he can play 15 ... ♘f4 and then after my reply 16 ♕g3 he has the rather unpleasant move 16 ... e5, which prevents me taking on g7 because my knight on c3 would be undefended. Unfortunately I didn't notice this move 16 ... e5 a couple of moves ago, so my ♗h5+ plan will now have to be abandoned. I'll fall back on my reserve scheme, which is to play e5.

14 e5

KASPAROV: In my opinion simply 14 0-0 was stronger. I would have played 14 ... ♕a5. Now I should play 14 ... dxe5 because 14 ... ♘d5 is very dangerous for me. He takes 15 ♘xd5 ♕a5+ and 16 ♕c3 ♕xd5 17 ♗f3 is bad for me. That's why I should take on e5. But now I have two extra pawns.

14 ...   dxe5
15 ♗xf6   gxf6

NUNN: By a curious transposition we've reached the game between Gavrikov and van der Wiel. Now I wish I could remember something about this. I do remember van der Wiel telling me that ♕d2 for White would have been a good move in some position. I can't exactly remember which position but I'm sure I'll be able to work it out when I get there.

Anyhow, there's only one consistent move here and that's to force Black to move his king by playing ♗h5+.

16 ♗h5+ ♔f8

NUNN: Perhaps ♕d2 is good here. I really want to put my knight on e4; this is the thing which is really going to make my attack strong. I can't do it at the moment because it allows exchange of queens. On the other hand after ♕d2 I threaten to give a rather nasty check on h6. He can stop that in various ways, but in any case I should be able to get my knight to e4 in a couple of moves and then I might get some genuine threats against his king. Of course I am two pawns down, and I haven't even castled yet, so the success of this is rather dubious.

17 ♕d2

KASPAROV: This is a new move. I am surprised. Van der Wiel played 17 0-0 and after 17 ... e4 18 ♕h3 f5 Gavrikov had a winning position. Now I should play 17 ... ♔g7, but what about 18 ♘d5 — it looks dangerous for me. Of course I can sacrifice the queen: 18 ... exd5 19 ♖b3 ♕xb3 and 20 ... ♗f5. It's good compensation, but there should be something stronger. Okay, 18 ♘d5 ♖d8 19 ♖b3 ♖xd5

20 ♖xa3 ♖xd2 21 ♖g3+ ♔h6 and I have a winning position. Okay, ♔g7. My position is very good and there are no direct threats from White's side.

17 ... ♔g7

18 ♖b3 ♕a5

NUNN: When my queen was on d3 the knight was pinned by the queen from a3; now that the queen's on d2, the knight's still pinned, so I don't seem able to get this knight to e4. I'll have to castle here and hope that I can get my knight to e4 in the next couple of moves.

19 0-0

KASPAROV: Rook g8 is a good move. In one move my king will be in the corner in a safe position and I can defend all the weaknesses on the kingside easily. I can be completely quiet now.

19 ... ♖g8

NUNN: It's starting to look a bit bad for me now. I can't quite see what I've got for my two pawns. If only I could get this rook on b3 over, I'd be okay, but I'm still in this pin. If I move my queen, then play the knight, then play the rook, that's three moves already. By that time Black will have been able to consolidate his defence perfectly. The best option is perhaps to play a move like ♔h1, so if Black plays ♔h8 at least

I can get my queen to h6 without loss of time. But I must admit I'm starting to have a rather bad feeling about this position.

| 20 | ♔h1 | ♔h8 |
| 21 | ♕h6 | |

KASPAROV: Okay, now the queen comes back to d8. The idea is ♕d8, ♕f8, f5 and all the strong pieces are around the king. The only chance for White is to make some threats on the kingside, but after ♕d8 and ♕f8 I see nothing.

| 21 | ... | ♕d8 |
| 22 | ♘e4 | f5 |

NUNN: He doesn't give me many chances. If I play 23 ♖d3, he can just play 23 ... ♗g5 forcing exchanges and leaving me a lot of material down. The only thing I can try for is some sort of trap here. Perhaps if I play 23 ♗f7, then if he took on e4, I might have some possibilities with ♕xe5+ and ♖h3. I'm sure my position is objectively lost, but I might as well try for one trick in any case.

| 23 | ♗f7 | |

KASPAROV: That looks like desperation; there's no threat at all. I can play, of course, ♕f8. It's the best move and I think he's going to play ♕h5. Then I can play ♖g4 or ♖g7 maybe. Those moves give me a winning position.

| 23 | ... | ♕f8 |
| 24 | ♕h5 | ♖g7 |

NUNN: Well, he didn't fall for the trap of taking on e4. I can play ♗e8 here and win the pawn on c6, but I'm still left one pawn down and the most serious defect of my position is now that his bishops are going to become extremely active. In fact my position appears to be not only materially worse but even worse from the strategic point of view. Well I'll play ♗e8, it's forced in any case.

| 25 | ♗e8 | a5 |
| 26 | ♗xc6 | |

KASPAROV: 26 ... ♗a6, then if 27 ♗xa8, ♗xf1 is winning. Maybe the best move is 27 ♗b5, then I can play 27 ... a4 28 ♖b1 ♗xb5 29 ♖xb5 ♕c8 winning again. Okay, ♗a6; I can't see a defence. If he plays ♖f2 or ♖f3 I play ♖d8 or ♖c8. It doesn't matter. I've an easy winning position.

| 26 | ... | ♗a6 |
| 27 | ♖f2 | ♖d8 |

NUNN: Well, it's time to survey the position. I'm a pawn down; my back rank is collapsing; my knight on e4 is about to drop off; and I am playing the world champion. Perhaps I'd better resign at this moment.

0:1

GAME THREE
KORCHNOI - HÜBNER

1 Nf3 d5 2 c4 c6 3 e3 Nf6 4 Nc3 e6 5 d4
Nbd7 6 Bd3 Bb4 7 a3 Ba5 8 0-0 0-0 9 Qc2
Qe7 10 cd ed 11 Bd2 Qd8 12 Ne2 Bb6 13
Ng3 Re8 14 b4 a6 15 Bc3 Nf8 16 Rae1
Be6 17 Ne5 N6d7 18 f4 f6 19 Nf3 Bc7 20
Nd2 Nb6 21 Ba1 Nf7 22 Nf5 Kh8 23 a4
Nc8 24 Nb3 Nd6 25 a5 Nxf5 26 Bxf5 Bd6
27 Bc3 Bg6 28 Bxg6 Nxg6 29 f5 Nf8 30 e4
Qc7 31 e5 fe 32 de Bxe5 33 Rxe5 Rxe5 34
f6 gf 35 Rxf6 Kg8 36 Qf2 Rae8 37 Rxf8+
Rxf8 38 Qg3+ Qg7 39 Qxg7+ Kxg7 40
Bxe5+ Kg6 41 Nc5 Re8 42 Bd4 Re2 43
Nxb7 Rd2 44 Be3 Rb2 45 Bc5 Kf5 46
Nd8 d4 47 Bxd4 Rxb4 48 Bb6 Rc4 49
Nb7 Kf4 50 Nc5 Rc1+ 51 Kf2 Rc2+ 52
Ke1 Rc1+ 53 Ke2 Rc2+ 54 Kd3 Rxg2 55
Nxa6 Ke5 56 Nc7 Rxh2 57 a6 Ra2 58 a7
Ra3+ 59 Ke2 Ra2+ 60 Kf3 Ra3+ 61 Be3
c5 62 a8Q Rxa8 63 Nxa8 c4 64 Nc7 1:0

GAME THREE

KORCHNOI - HÜBNER

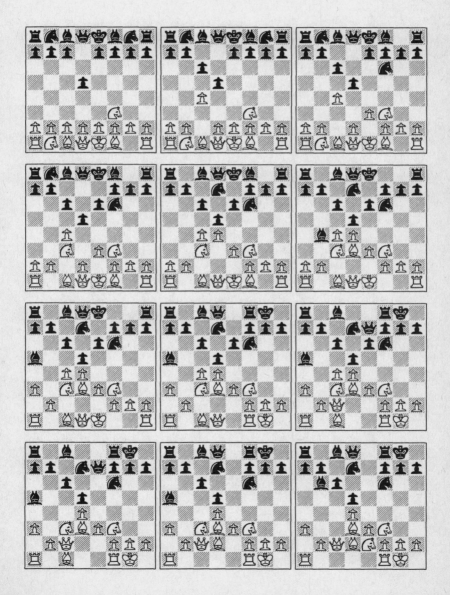

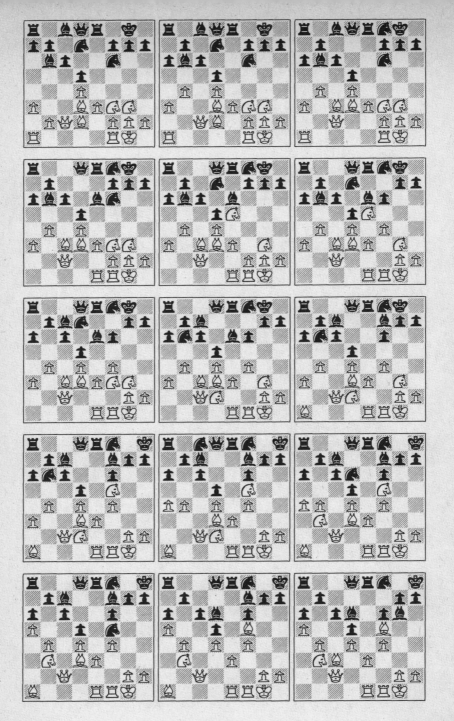

26

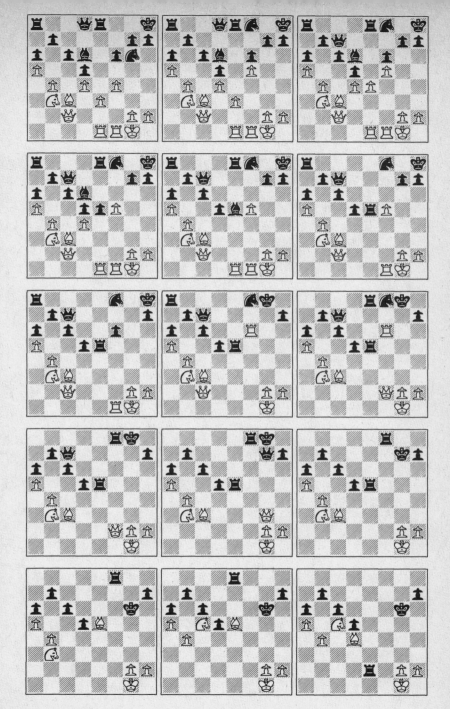

27

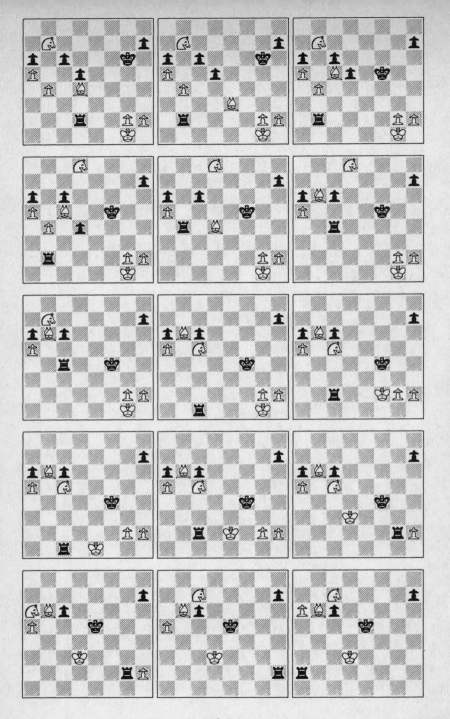

28

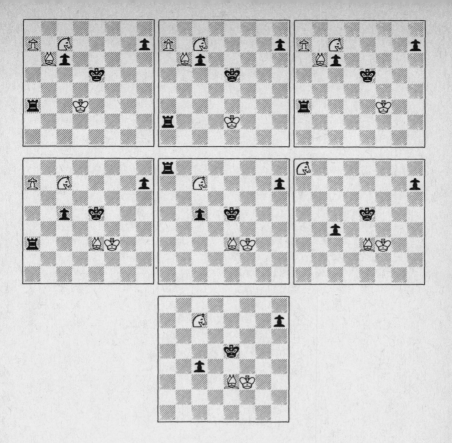

1:0

Korchnoi - Hübner

1	♘f3	d5
2	c4	c6
3	e3	♘f6
4	♘c3	e6
5	d4	♘bd7
6	♗d3	♗b4
7	a3	

7 0-0 0-0 8 ♗d2 ♕e7 (8 ... dc 9 ♗xc4 ♗d6 10 ♕c2 e5 11 ♖ae1 ♕e7 is Larsen - Flear London 1986.) 9 a3 ♗d6 10 c5 ♗c7 11 e4 de 12 ♗xe4 ♘xe4 13 ♘xe4 ♖d8 14 ♕c1 ♘f8 was in Portisch -Hübner, Tilburg 1986.

7 ...   ♗a5!?

Inviting White to set up a Q-side bind in due course with b4. In a later round Hübner was to try 7 ... Ba5 against Kasparov (see game 24) and lost ignominiously. It seems that 6 ... ♗b4, the invention of the Italian Master Ronih, frowned on ever since 1948, really is inferior.

8	0-0	0-0
9	♕c2	♕e7
10	cxd5	

Forestalling Black's possible plan of ... dxc4 and ... e5. After 10 ♗d2 dxc4 11 ♗xc4 e5 12 ♖ae1 ♗c7 13 ♘e4 Botvinnik - Euwe World Ch. 1948 is reached, which is considered in White's favour.

10 . . .   exd5

10 ... cxd5 11 b4 ♗b6 (11 ... ♗c7?! 11 ... ♗d8?!) 12 ♘a4 gives White a tremendous initiative.

11 ♗d2 ♕d8

An unpleasant move, but White threatened ♘xd5, and if 11 ... ♗b6 12 ♘a4 ♗c7 13 ♗b4 ♗d6 14 ♗xd6 ♕xd6 15 b4 with an accel-erated minority attack. 11 ... ♗c7 fails to 12 ♘b5! while 11 ... ♗d8 is too congested and 11 ... ♗xc3 prematurely surrenders Black's KB. So there is method in Hübner's apparent madness.

12 ♘e2 ♗b6

Hübner is anxious *not* to exchange his valuable dark-squared bishop of White's

QB, which is somewhat hemmed in by its own pawns.

13 ♘g3   ♖e8
14 b4   a6
15 ♗c3   ♘f8
16 ♖ae1

Korchnoi masses his pieces for a K-side attack, having first secured the queen's wing against possible counterplay. Hübner's conduct of the opening has been very subtle, but he has lost a lot of time (3 moves with his KB, 2 with his Q out of 15 so far played).

16 ...   ♗e6
17 ♘e5   ♘6d7
18 f4

The good old Pillsbury Attack.

18 ...   f6
19 ♘f3   ♗c7
20 ♘d2

Having been chased from c5, White's N makes for the alternate outpost on c5.

20 ...   ♘b6
21 ♗a1   ♗f7
22 ♘f5   ♔h8
23 a4   ♘c8
24 ♘b3   ♘d6
25 a5

So, b7 is fixed as a weakness, and c5 is secured for White's N; all this at the price of a N exchange on the K-side which somewhat relieves Black's swap.

25 ...   ♘xf5
26 ♗xf5   ♗d6

27 ♗c3   ♗g6
28 ♗xg6   ♘xg6
29 f5   ♘f8

Hübner's play is positionally impeccable as he gradually swaps off White's aggressive pieces and avoids weaknesses, but all the time White is gradually encroaching on him, gaining time and space.

30 e4   ♕c7

30 ... dxe4 31 ♖xe4 ♕d7!? may be a better defence. The text allows a tactical trick.

31 e5!

A coup which either establishes a mighty central passed pawn (after 31 ... ♗e7) or leads Black into a perilous labyrinth of tactical complications, with Black's King at the wrong end of White's QB. Normally Korchnoi shuns Tal-like speculations of this sort, but Hübner was probably short of time.

31 ...   fxe5

Nevertheless Hübner opts for the labyrinth.

32	dxe5	♗xe5
33	♖xe5!	♖xe5
34	f6!	

Smashing the barricades along the vitally important a1-h8 diagonal; 34 ... g6 fails to 35 f7 with an eternal pin against the Black Rook, but 34 ... ♖g5 or 34 ... ♘g6 both look playable.

34	...	gxf6
35	♖xf6	♔g8
36	♕f2	

The climax. Black must play 36 ... ♘g6 when White has practical chances after 37 ♘c5 ♖ae8. Instead, Hübner blunders. His next move is plausible, but it invites a fearsome continuation. If you have not already seen it, try covering the page with some paper and work out for yourself Korchnoi's combination after Black's next move ...

36	...	♖ae8?
37	♖xf8+!	♖xf8

38	♕g3+

Wins the exposed Rook on e5.

38	...	♕g7
39	♕xg7+	♔xg7
40	♗xe5+	♔g6
41	♘c5	♖e8
42	♗d4	♖e2

The passive 42 ... ♖e7 allows White to push forward his K-side pawn majority at his leisure. Hübner seeks to confuse the issue.

43	♘xb7	♖d2
44	♗e3	♖b2
45	♗c5	♔f5
46	♘d8	d4
47	♗xd4	♖b4
48	♗b6	♖c4
49	♘b7	

The problem for Black is that his pawn on a6 is doomed. Therefore, the two pieces are clearly superior to the Rook.

49	...	♔f4
50	♘c5	♖c1+
51	♔f2	♖c2+
52	♔e1	♖c1+

53	♔e2	♖c2+		62	a8♕	♖xa8
54	♔d3	♖xg2		63	♘xa8	c4
55	♘xa6	♔e5		64	♘c7	
56	♘c7	♖xh2				
57	a6	♖a2				
58	a7	♖a3+				
59	♔e2	♖a2+				
60	♔f3	♖a3+				
61	♗e3	c5				

Black resigns.

There is no point speculating on Korchnoi's ability to win with B+N v R!

OFF THE BOARD

Another visitor to Brussels, also staying at the Hyatt Regency Hotel, was United States Secretary of State George Schultz.

Eventually his path crossed with that of Kasparov and several photographers got the 'George meets Gary' picture. However, although everyone was clear that the two men conversed, no-one was too sure what they actually talked about.

While it would have been interesting to report Kasparov's opinions on 'Star Wars' or Schultz's views on Soviet world chess domination, the truth is that they spoke for some two minutes in English without discussing anything more controversial than the morning's weather forecast.

The only other meeting with wider implications occured in the Swiss tournament, where the 20 competitors included six grandmasters, when England's Malcolm Pein sat down to play Garcia Palermo of Argentina.

The Belgian Press recalled quite recent events in the South Atlantic but no blood was spilt at the chessboard, the game being drawn.

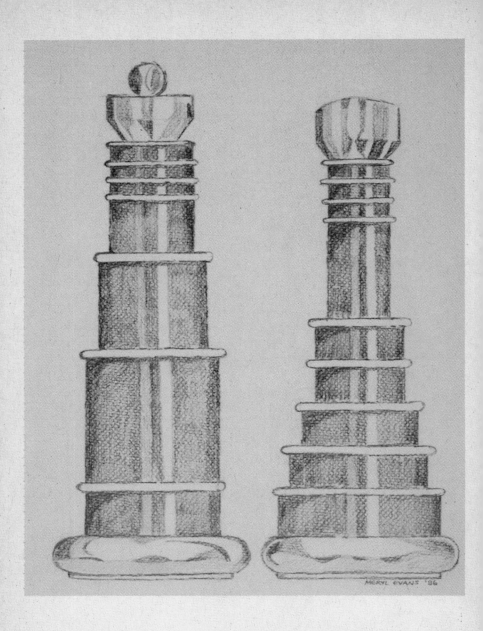

ROUND TWO:

Game No.4	Short	1:0	Hübner
Game No.5	Kasparov	½:½	Korchnoi
Game No.6	Portisch	½:½	Nunn

As in the first round, it was Portisch's game which brought a bit of grandmasterly decorum to another day of otherwise unaccustomed excitement. Kasparov-Korchnoi was the highlight, bringing the audience to their feet in applause when the draw was agreed. It had been a most remarkable game, in which Kasparov was forced to exercise his most imaginative abilities in order to conjure up a swindle to save himself from the results of earlier impetuous sacrifices.

Compared with that game, Short-Hübner might have seemed a quiet game, but by any normal standards it too was full of interest. Hübner missed the correct defence against a speculative piece sacrifice by Short (After the game the players analysed 13 ... ♘bd7 as better for Black) and later even blundered (32 ... ♗f5?) but still put a magnificent fight in the endgame. Short's fluctuating emotions in this game are revealed by his television commentary, which makes a fascinating contrast with Raymond Keene's objective notes to the game.

SCORES: Kasparov, Short & Korchnoi 1½;
Portisch 1, Nunn ½, Hübner 0.

GAME FOUR
SHORT - HÜBNER

1 e4 c5 2 Nf3 d6 3 d4 cd 4 Nxd4 Nf6 5 Nc3 a6 6 Be3 e6 7 Qd2 b5 8 f3 Bb7 9 0-0-0 Nbd7 10 g4 Nb6 11 h4 Rc8 12 Ncxb5 ab 13 Bxb5+ Nfd7 14 Qb4 Qc7 15 Qb3 Kd8 16 Bg5+ Be7 17 Bxd7 Kxd7 18 Nb5 Qc4 19 Nxd6 Qxb3 20 Nxc8+ Kxc8 21 ab f6 22 Bf4 Bc6 23 Nd6 Bd8 24 h5 f5 25 gf ef 26 Rhg1 Rg8 27 Rd4 fe 28 fe Be8 29 h6 g5 30 Rg3 g4 31 e5 Nd7 32 Bc5 Nf5 33 Rxd8+ Kxd8 34 Bxb6+ Kd7 35 c4 Ne6 36 Kd2 Rg6 37 Be3 Kxe5 38 Kc3 Ne4 39 b4 Bf3 40 b5 Ke4 41 Bc1 Rd6 42 Rg1 Be2 43 Re1 Kf3 44 Bf4 Re6 45 Bc7 Bxc4 46 Rxe6 Bxe6 47 Kd4 Bc8 48 Kc5 Ke4 49 Bg3 Kf5 50 Kc6 Kg5 51 b6 Bf5 52 b7 Be4+ 53 Kc7 Bxb7 54 Kxb7 Kxh6 55 b4 Kg5 56 b5 h5 57 b6 h4 58 Bd6 g3 59 Ka6 h3 60 Bxg3 1:0

GAME FOUR

SHORT - HÜBNER

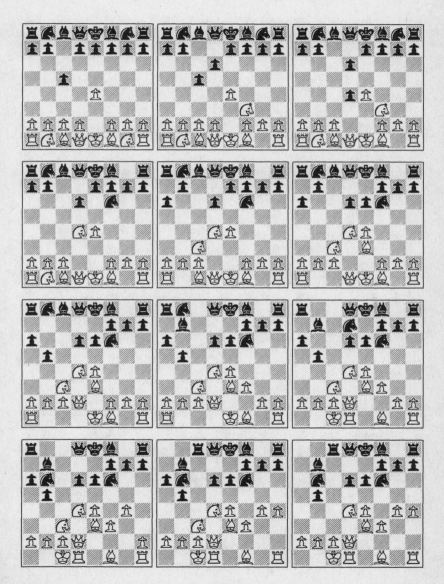

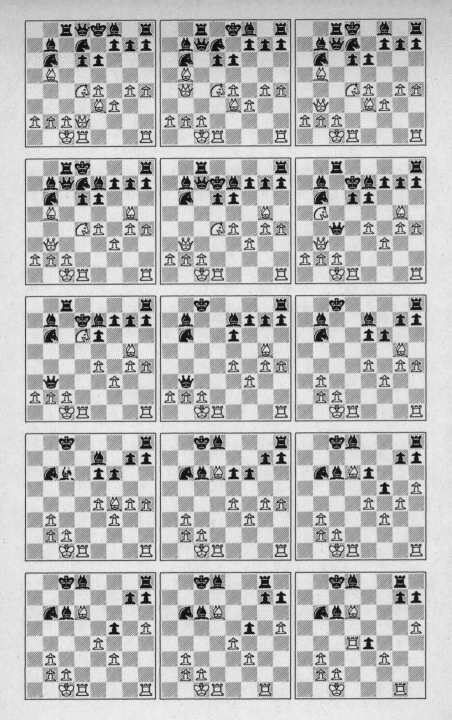

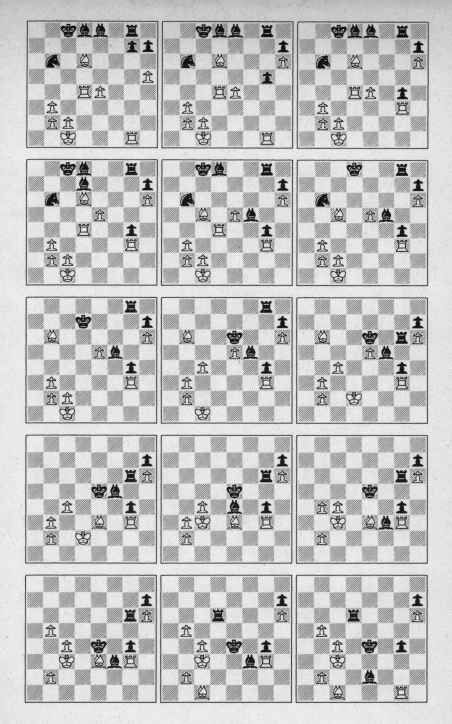

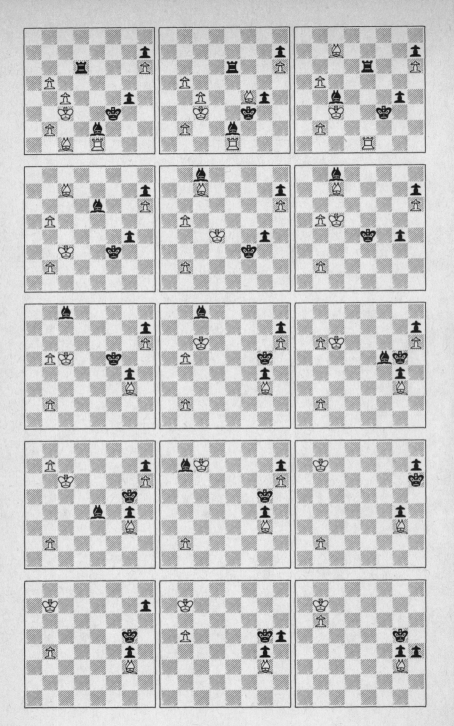

40

1:0

Robert Hübner, already deep in thought.

Short - Hübner

1	e4	c5
2	♘f3	d6
3	d4	cxd4
4	♘xd4	♘f6
5	♘c3	a6
6	♗e3	

6 ♗g5 is beginning to look less convincing in view of the revival of the Poison Pawn variation. See, for example, Kasparov's demolition of John Nunn in round one. 6 ♗e3 is Short's favourite and is considerably less well documented than most alternatives against the Najdorf.

6	...	e6
7	♕d2	b5
8	f3	♗b7
9	0-0-0	♘bd7

White's strategy is relatively simple, if hard to meet. Short overprotects the pawn on e4 in preparation for a storm on the King's flank with his g and h pawns. As in so many contemporary versions of the Sicilian, Black at first neglects his overall development in favour of establishing an aggressive Q-side configuration.

10	g4	♘b6

Eyeing c4, and making room for the KN to retreat to d7.

11	h4	♖c8?

This is too provocative. Black should take time off to develop at least some of his kingside pieces with 11 ... ♗e7!

12	♘cxb5!	axb5
13	♗xb5+	♘fd7
14	♕b4	

This is a typical sacrifice, to be found also in games by

Capablanca and Karpov. White gains a mass of pawns for the piece, plus attacking chances, and a substantial lead in development. The reason that such sacrifices are difficult to judge correctly is that Black may create a counterattack in the c-file, and White's passed pawns cannot easily be advanced in the middle game since they are in front of his own King. If now 14 ... d5 opening fire on White's Q then 15 ♕b3! leaves Black too open.

14 ...   ♕c7
15 ♕b3

Threatening to win with 16 ♘xe6!

15 ...   ♔d8
16 ♗g5+   ♗e7
17 ♗xd7   ♔xd7
18 ♘b5   ♕c4
19 ♘xd6!!

A splendid sacrifice. If now 19 ... ♗xd6 20 ♖xd6+ ♔xd6 21 ♕xb6+ followed by the deadly ♖d1+

Hübner is therefore obliged to seek refuge in a most inferior endgame.

19 ...   ♕xb3
20 ♘xc8+   ♔xc8
21 axb3   f6
22 ♗f4   ♗c6
23 ♗d6   ♗d8
24 h5   f5

Black strives to open lines for his Bishop before he is squashed by an onrush of White Q-side pawn phalanx.

25 gxf5   exf5
26 ♖hg1   ♖g8
27 ♖d4   fxe4
28 fxe4   ♗e8
29 h6   g5

Black's counter-action had led to the creation of a passed pawn. Pinning his hopes on this pawn the German just succeeds in putting up a brave rearguard action.

30 ♖g3   g4
31 e5   ♗d7
32 ♗c5   ♗f5!?

43

Was this move a blunder? The most solid move here is 32 ... ♖g6. The text loses 2 minor pieces for a Rook to an extremely modest combination. The upshot is that White stays several pawns ahead in an ending of Rook and opposite-coloured Bishops. Nevertheless, Black's passed g-pawn, active K, and the weakness of the White pawns on e5 and h6 still conspire to grant Black chances for a draw.

33	♖xd8+	♔xd8
34	♗xb6+	♔d7
35	c4	♔e6
36	♔d2	

White cannot hold both e5 and h6. He sensibly decides to defend h6, thus preventing Black from obtaining connected passed pawns of his own.

36	...	♖g6
37	♗e3	♔xe5
38	♔c3	♗e4
39	b4	♗f3
40	b5	♔e4
41	♗c1	♖d6

A neat trick to activate his B. If 44 ... ♔xf4 45 ♖xe2 wins easily.

44	...	♖e6
45	♗c7	

With the threat of b6, so Black must permit the final liquidation.

45	...	♗xc4
46	♖xe6	♗xe6
47	♔d4	♗c8
48	♔c5	♔e4

White's reserve b-pawn is now the decisive factor. Hübner races his K round to capture the pawn on h6, but he is not in time.

49	♗g3	♔f5
50	♔c6	♔g5
51	b6	♗f5
52	b7	♗e4+
53	♔c7	♗xb7
54	♔xb7	♔xh6
55	b4	♔g5
56	b5	h5
57	b6	h4
58	♗d6	g3

59	♔a6	h3
60	♗xg3	

Black resigns.

Black might have spared himself the last few moves. This is the type of game which encourages Nigel's supporters to regard him as the possibly leading Western contender to challenge for the world title.

OFF THE BOARD

The OHRA tournament organisers had to handle one or two strange requests. Among these was a letter to ex-world champion Bobby Fischer from one of his Belgian fans.

Roughly translated, this read: "Dear Bobby, I am so glad you are playing at OHRA as I have long been trying to contact you for your autograph. Would you please let me have this?"

After making discreet enquiries to check that they were not the victims of a hoax, the organisers approached the reigning world champion whereupon a reply went back with Kasparov's autograph instead.

No more was heard of the matter so it was assumed that this proved a satisfactory substitute.

— The Players TV commentaries

(When approached by the tournament organisers before the start of the event, Robert Hübner had expressed some reluctance towards committing himself to giving comment for television. The BBC agreed to respect his naturally cautious attitude towards publicity, so the Hübner games always appeared on the screens with a one-sided view. On the present occasion, the emotional character of a chess game came through well in Nigel's solo version).

Phase One
Short gives in to temptation

1	e4	c5
2	♘f3	d6
3	d4	cxd4
4	♘xd4	♘f6
5	♘c3	a6
6	♗e3	e6
7	♕d2	b5
8	f3	♗b7
9	0-0-0	♘bd7
10	g4	♘b6
11	h4	♖c8

SHORT: Well, this guy is really tempting me here. With his previous move 10 ... ♘b6 we've entered territory which I don't know anything about. I assume he analysed this before, but his knight on b6 is a little bit of a tactical weakness here. I'm tempted to play a move like ♕f2 intending ♘xe6, but I guess he would just remove his knight from the kingside with ♘fd7, then he's got ideas of ♘c4 or b4. You name it - he's got ideas here.

I am very tempted by the fact that he's two moves away from castling here. I have an interesting idea just to take on b5 with my knight on c3, and if he recaptures, then ♗xb5+. If then ♘bd7, I have g5 with some initiative, and it's an awkward pin. His other possibility (after ♗xb5+) is to play ♘fd7 and then I really do attack his knight on b6. I play ♕b4, threatening just ♗xd7+ and also threatening ♘xe6. In fact these tactical possibilities are really very awkward for him to meet. There's another factor which is coming into consideration here - I've already used up quite a lot of time. I think from a practical point of view, I should just sacrifice the knight and ... what the hell!

Phase Two
Cause for optimism

12	♘cxb5	axb5
13	♗xb5+	♘fd7
14	♕b4	♕c7
15	♕b3	♔d8

SHORT: King d8, my goodness! This is really asking for trouble. I mean ♗xd7 is very strong here. But I'm tempted by this move ♗g5+. What does he do then? He can't return his king to e8 because of ♘xe6; and f6 allows ♘xe6; and ♘f6 allows e5. Well, I guess ♕e7 is his only move, but then his d-pawn will be dropping off. I'm really quite surprised but,

well, I can't complain here.
Phase Three
It looks like a winning position.

16	♗g5+	♗e7
17	♗xd7	♔xd7
18	♘b5	♕c4
19	♘xd6	♕xb3
20	♘xc8+	♔xc8
21	axb3	f6

SHORT: I'm slightly surprised by the turn of events because really it's been very easy for me. I sacrificed a piece for two pawns and a check - which is always adequate compensation in my eyes - but now surely this is just a winning position. I mean three pawns, they must decide the day. I can see that it may be a little bit tricky here because he has two bishops and I imagine he's going to do everything possible to preserve them. If I can exchange a pair of bishops his defence will collapse almost instantly, so this is really my problem. If I play

47

♗e3 to gain a tempo, his knight comes to d7 and to e5. I still have some weaknesses with my kingside pawns. But I have another more attractive possibility, just to put my bishop on f4, then if he plays e5 he will have taken this square from his knight. So ♗f4, intending ♗d6. This is my objective: to exchange a pair of bishops and then let my pawns decide the day.

Phase Four
Doubts begin to set in.

22	♗f4	♗c6
23	♗d6	♗d8
24	h5	f5
25	gxf5	exf5
26	♖hg1	♖g8
27	♖d4	fxe4
28	fxe4	♗e8
29	h6	g5

SHORT: I've got a terrible feeling that I lost control of this position. The bishops sitting on the back row are remarkable in their defensive possibilities. My pawn on h6 is weak now. He has ♖g6 hitting it and his g-pawn advancing up the board. I can't help thinking that I should have had some much easier way. I'm not sure what but this whole endgame has been very difficult - much more difficult than I imagined when he first went into it. He's generated a lot of play and not only that, but I'm running short of time. Ten moves in ten minutes, and the position is extremely complicated. I don't quite know what to do. I've got four passed pawns, but where are they going? It's not so easy to advance these guys. I want to play c4, but he has, well, g4 or ♖g6, many possibilities. The clock's ticking away. I don't know; maybe if I try and swing my rook over to the queenside, ♖g3. This gives me some possibilities of ♖c3+. I don't know exactly, I haven't time to calculate it properly.

Phase Five
"He's really screwed it up. The game's as good as over."

30	♖g3	g4
31	e5	♗d7
32	♗c5	♗f5
33	♖xd8+	♔xd8
34	♗xb6+	♔d7

SHORT: It looks like he's really screwed it up here. I was surprised because this ending was very difficult, but now it must be very easy for me. Three connected passed pawns on the queenside, that must decide it. he has only one dangerous pawn, on g4, and that's firmly blockaded. it seems that I just get my pawns going a little bit, then that's it. I mean, the game's as good as over. Very simple, c4 here.

Phase Six
Perhaps not so easy after all.

35	c4	♔e6
36	♔d2	♖g6
37	♗e3	♔xe5
38	♔c3	♗e4
39	b4	♗f3
40	b5	♔e4
41	♗c1	♖d6
42	♖g1	♗e2

SHORT: I'm not sure how I could have played this better. My moves seem to have been fairly logical so

a hell of a lot of counterplay. His king is coming to f3, king f2, then g3, g2. Well, Okay, I have two extra pawns here. This ought to be easy enough, but I can't help feeling there ought to have been something easier. My pieces are lacking coordination, but even so there ought to be a fairly simple way of winning here. I have one idea: just to play 43 ♖e1, then after 43 ... ♔f3 just to play 44 ♖xe2 and 45 ♗f4. My pawns are so strong on the queenside, they ought eventually to decide the day. But there's another way of playing. After 43 ♖e1 ♔f3 I can play 44 ♗f4 first. I guess that ought still to leave me with a winning position. But it's very odd because this whole ending ought to have been trivially winning for me and this guy's making me find difficult ideas all the time.

49

Phase Seven
Oversight, near panic, and a win by one tempo.

43	♖e1	♔f3
44	♗f4	♖e6
45	♗c7	♗xc4
46	♖xe6	♗xe6
47	♔d4	♗c8
48	♔c5	♔e4
49	♗g3	♔f5
50	♔c6	♔g5

SHORT: Christ! I didn't even notice that move was legal. It's incredible how I've been playing this game. Just like I've been in a trance. For some reason I was only considering ♔g6 when I play ♗f4. This is ridiculous. Maybe he has some drawing chances here. My h-pawn is going and he has two connected passed pawns. ... Let's just hold on a minute. I suppose it's just a simple matter of calculation. I play b6, he has to play 51 ... ♗f5, otherwise I play ♔c7 and my pawn does queen. Then I move my king, 52 ... ♗e4, 53 b7, ♗xb7 54 ♔xb7, ♔xh6, my pawn moves, his king moves, my pawn, his pawn ... god, what's happening here. I can't think, I'm so tired, it's such a long session. So difficult, I have to look at this again. His pawn gets to h4, then I move by bishop, then g3, I move my king. Good. This is just winning. By one tempo. Incredible, the way I've played. But anyway, it looks like the point is still in the bag.

51	b6	♗f5
52	b7	♗e4+
53	♔c7	♗xb7
54	♔xb7	♔xh6
55	b4	♔g5
56	b5	h5
57	b6	h4
58	♗d6	g3
59	♔a6	h3
60	♗xg3	
1:0		

GAME FIVE
KASPAROV-KORCHNOI

1 d4 Nf6 2 c4 e6 3 Nf3 Bb4+ 4 Bd2 c5 5 g3 Qb6 6 Bg2 Nc6 7 d5 ed 8 cd Nxd5 9 0-0 Nde7 10 e4 d6 11 Be3 Qc7 12 a3 Ba5 13 Bf4 Ne5 14 b4 cb 15 ab Bxb4 16 Qa4+ N7c6 17 Nd4 a5 18 Nc3 Bd7 19 Nd5 Qd8 20 Nf5 0-0 21 Qd1 Bc5 22 Rc1 a4 23 g4 a3 24 g5 a2 25 Qh5 Bxf5 26 ef Bd4 27 Bxe5 Nxe5 28 Be4 Re8 29 Rc7 a1Q 30 Rxa1 Rxa1+ 31 Kg2 Ra2 32 Re7 Rxf2+ 33 Kg3 Rxe7 34 f6 Ng6 35 Nxe7+ Kf8 36 Qxh7 Bxf6 37 Nxg6+ fg 38 Kxf2 Qb6+ 39 Kg2 Qb2+ 40 Kh3 Bxg5 41 Qxg6 Qf6 42 Qxf6+ ½:½

GAME FIVE

KASPAROV · KORCHNOI

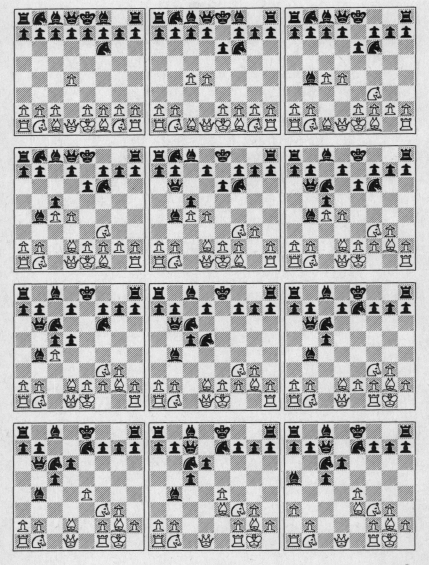

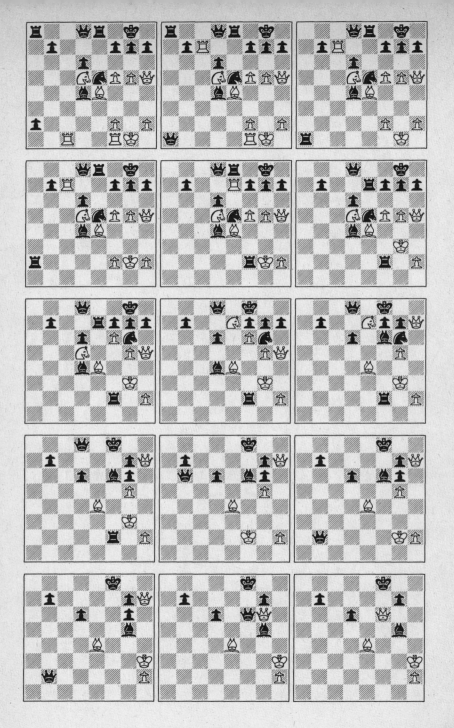

Kasparov - Korchnoi

The game which follows is incredible and dramatic. Kasparov sacrifices two pawns speculatively, then two rooks, even more so, and still draws. It reminds me of some of Alekhine's berserk attacks. I have always maintained that Alekhine's fiery spirit lives on in Kasparov. I have even heard it said that Alekhine has been reincarnated in Kasparov! Maybe - for then who believes in such things.

Of the three old giants, Lasker, Capablanca and Alekhine, only Alekhine revelled in such wild experimental adventures. Just compare these three games of his for sheer speculative bravado:

Euwe - Alekhine, 1935 World Ch. (12)
1 d4 Nf6 2 c4 g6 3 Nc3 d5 4 Qb3 dc 5 Qxc4 Bg7 6 e4 0-0 7 Nf3 a6 8 Bf4 b5! 9 Qxc7 Qe8? 10 Be2 Nc6 11 d5 Nb4?! 12 0-0 Nxe4 13 Nxe4 Nxd5 1-0 36

Alekhine - Euwe, World Ch. 1935 (25)
Alekhine even experimented when his world title hung in the balance!

1 d4 d5 2 c4 c6 3 Nf3 Nf6 4 Nc3 e6 5 Bg5 Nbd7 6 e3 Qa5 7 cd Nxd5 8 Qd2 N7b6 9 Bd3 Nxc3 10 bc Nd5 11 Rc1 Nxc3 12 0-0 Bb4 13 a3 Qxa3 14 Ra1 Qb3 15 Bc2 Qd5 16 e4 Nxe4 17 Qxb4 Nxg5 18 Ne5 a5 19 Qa3 f6 20 Bg6+?! hg 21 Nxg6 Nf3+! 0-1 40

Euwe - Alekhine, 1937 World Ch. (19)
1 d4 Nf6 2 c4 e6 3 Nc3 Bb4 4 Nf3 Ne4 5 Qc2 d5 6 e3 c5 7 Bd3 Nf6 8 cd ed 9 dc Bxc5 10 0-0 Nc6 11 e4 Be7 12 e5 Ng4 13 Re1 Bb4 14 Bb5+ Kf8 15 Qe2 Bc5 16 Nd1 Bf5 17 h3 h5 ½-½ 49

Only half a point for this effort, but Alekhine is still admired for his courage.

1	d4	Nf3
2	c4	e6
3	Nf3	Bb4+
4	Bd2	c5

A few years ago everybody said: "5 Bxb4 cxb4 with advantage to White", since the c5 pawn vanishes away from the centre. Now, we realise that White cannot develop his QN to c3, it's best square, so this dogmatic verdict is not so clear. Van der Sterren - Seirawan, Wijk aan Zee 1986 5 ♗xb4 cb 6 g3 0-0 7 ♘g2 d6 8 0-0 a5 9 ♘bd2 ♘bd7 10 a3 ba 11 ♖xa3 ♕c7 12 ♘e1 e5 illustrates this. Belyavsky -Seirawan, Montpellier 1985, had proceeded 5 ♗xb4 cb 6 a3! ba 7 ♖xa3 d6 8 e3 0-0 9 ♗e2 b6 10 0-0 a5 11 b4 ♘c6 12 ba ♘xa5 13 ♘c3! + =.

5 g3 ♕b6!?

Korchnoi is a sly old fox. He tempts Kasparov with something unsound with this provocative Queen sortie.

6 ♗g2

6 a3 is not initiative-seeking; eg. 6 ... ♗xd2+ 7 ♕xd2 ♘c6 8 dc ♕xc5 9 e3 0-0 10 ♘c3 b6 11 b4 ♕h5 12 ♗e2 ♗b7 13 e4 ♖fd8 is Thorsteins - Kir. Georgiev, Kiljava 1984.

6 ... ♘c6

After Kasparov's world title game everyone knows about tries like 6 ... cd 7 ♘xd4! ♕xd4 8 ♗xb4.

Of more than just curiosity is Djurić - J. Horvath, Szirak 1985, which went 6 ... cd 7 ♘xd4 ♗c5 8 ♗c3 e5 9 b4 ♗xd4 0-1!; the gambit 8 e3 is more likely to appeal to Kasparov.

The test continues provoking the world champion, who would not like to play the passive 7 e3.

7 d5 ed
8 cd ♘xd5
9 0-0 ♘de7
10 e4

White has a lead in development, play against Black's exposed Q and pressure on the d-file for his sacrificed pawn.

10 ... d6
11 ♗e3

11 ♗f4 deserves consideration, probably met by 11 ... ♘d4.

11 ... ♕c7
12 a3 ♗a5
13 ♗f4 ♘e5
14 b4!?

White must confuse the issue. Black threatens to consolidate with ... ♘7g6, and if White plays ♘c3 Black just lops it off with ... ♗xc3!

14 ... cb
15 ab ♗xb4
16 ♕a4+ ♘7c6

17	♘d4	a5
18	♘c3	

At last White can develop his QN to its 'best square', but at the cost of two pawns. If now 18 ... ♗xc3 19 ♘b5!

18	...	♗d7
19	♘d5	♛d8
20	♘f5	0-0
21	♛d1	

Typical Kasparov, they say, but he must, in any case get his Q away from the diagonal of Black's QB. But ♛a4 (b3 or c2) to d1 occurs so often in Kasparov games. One idea is to attack Black's King, which has usually fled to the K-side. Soon, very soon, ♛h5 comes.

21	...	♗c5
22	♖c1	a4

Korchnoi, very sensibly, advances his passed a-pawn. Black is two connected passed pawns up and is, of course, winning. It is remarkable that Kasparov got any chances at all. At the start of these notes I showed three Alekhine games. One could also compare the second game of Kasparov's first match with Karpov.

23	g4	a3
24	g5	a2
25	♛h5	

White's plight is so desperate that there is even an argument for 25 ♘xg7 ♛xg7 26 ♛h5. This whole scenario reminds me of Reti's imaginative description of a similar situation (slow King's attack in competition with massive Q-side superiority) from a game Pillsbury -Tarrasch, Hasting 1895: "We are all familiar with the film dramas, in which the hero or heroine is in imminent danger of death, whilst at the same time other developments are taking place with a view to rescue ..." (eg. heroine tied to rails, while fast, enormous locomotive approaches ...) "The audience follows the action and counteraction in breathless suspense, for to all appearances the rescuer will arrive on the scene too late. Only at the very last moment, when all hope has been abandoned, is the tragic end averted." (*Masters of the Chess Board*).

25	...	♗xf5
26	ef	♗d4
27	♗xe5	♘xe5

It looks as if the game is up. Black's B on d4 covers a1 and defends f6 and g7 in reserve; (eg. 28 f6 ♘g6).

28 ♗e4

Threatening 29 f6 ♘g6 30 ♘e7+ ♚h3 31 ♗xg6 which Korchnoi takes off time to prevent, before executing his own devastating threat of ... a1=♕.

28 ... ♖e8
29 ♖c7 a1♕
30 ♖xa1 ♖xa1 +
31 ♚g2 ♖a2

Why not? Surely White must now capitulate.

32 ♖e7

This cannot work, but it is a brilliant try. Alekhine would have been proud of it.

32 ... ♖xf2 +

It is not clear that this is necessary. Maybe Black could continue as in the game, but with his R on a2, a safe square. Anyway, capturing another pawn with check should be good in time trouble.

33 ♚g3 ♖xe7

Winning another Rook. But why not 33 ... ♕a8? eg. 34 ♖xe8+ ♕xe8 35 f6 ♘g6, or 34 f6 ♕a3 + and Black wins.

34 f6 ♘g6

34 ... g6? loses, eg. 35 ♕h6 ♕f8 36 ♘xe7 + .

35 ♘xe7 + ♚f8

Not 35 ... ♘xe7 36 ♕xh7+ ♚f8 37 ♕h8+ ♘g8 38 ♕xg7+ ♚e8 39 ♕xg8+ ♚d7 40 ♕xf7+ ♚c8 41 ♕xb7 mate; 35 ... ♚h8 also looks extremely dangerous after 36 ♗xg6 fg 37 ♘xg6+ ♚g8 38 ♘e7+ ♚f8 39 ♕xh7, or 36 fxg7+ ♚xg7 37 ♕h6+ ♚h8 38 ♗xg6 fxg6 39 ♘xg6+ ♚g8, but even in these lines Black is probably winning. (*A. Martin*)

36 ♕xh7

If 36 ♗xg6 (hoping for 36 ... fg 37 ♕xh7) then 36 ... ♗xg6! is confusing but strong: (37 ♚xf2 ♕xe7 38 gf ♕xf6+ 39 ♗f5 g6 40 ♕h8+ ♚g8 etc ...)

36 ... ♗xf6

Another chance missed! 36 ... ♖xf6! was correct. eg 37 gxf6 (37 ♘d5 ♖f5!) ♗xf6 38 ♘xg6+ fxg6 39 ♗xg6 d5 and Black should win. (*A. Martin*)

37 ♘xg6+ fg

38 &xf2

The position is chaotic -both players are in desperate time trouble. White has been two Rooks down, gets one back, saw he can take another. Maybe that's a mistake. After 38 &d5 I don't see Black's win, eg. 38 ... ♛b6 39 ♛g8+ ♚e7 40 gf+ gf 41 ♛f7+ ♚d8 42

♛g8+ ♚c7 43 ♛f7+ ♚b8 44 ♛e8+ ♚a7 45 ♛a4+ draw! Black has alternatives on move 38. I still don't see a win. If it's there, I am happy for someone to show me.

38 ... ♛b6+
39 ♚g2 ♛b2+
40 ♚h3 &xg5?

Surely 40 ... &c5!

41 ♛xg6 ♛f6?

Korchnoi must have lost track of how many moves had been made. 41 ... &f6 (two pawns up, White's King exposed) must keep chances.

42 ♛xf6+

Played with 'both hands'. 42 ... &xf6 43 &xb7 when White can easily blockade the d-pawn. So, DRAW!

What a game.

KASPAROV-KORCHNOI   Rd 2

— The Players TV commentaries

1	d4	♞f6
2	c4	e6
3	♞f3	♝b4+
4	♝d2	

KORCHNOI: I had anticipated that my partner would play this way and I had prepared at home the move c5. I have some interesting ideas around this move, so I thought that I would take him aback.

| 4 | ... | c5 |
| 5 | g3 | ♛b6 |

KASPAROV: Okay, Korchnoi plays very fast, so maybe he specially prepares something for this game. ♛b6 must be a new move. There are many threats. I should think about my centre. ♝g2 should be the normal move. If he plays ♞c6 I have a chance to play a gambit with d5. It should be interesting. It's something like my game with Spassky in the Olympics.

| 6 | ♝g2 | ♞c6 |

KASPAROV: Okay, now I should sacrifice something. It's no pleasure to give a pawn or two pawns to Korchnoi at the beginning of a game, but what can I do? 7 d5 looks the best move — maybe just one pawn and many active opportunities.

| 7 | d5 | |

KORCHNOI: He didn't have any other choice. It's a long time since I last played Kasparov. I always had the feeling that he makes his sacrifices with full knowledge and full confidence of getting the initiative. But now when I look at his face it doesn't seem so. Well, he's sacrificing because of a bad life, because, well, it's the only chance for him not to lose the game. I have analysed this position. I am not afraid. I take.

7	...	exd5
8	cxd5	♞xd5
9	0-0	♞de7
10	e4	d6

KASPAROV: After 11 ♝f4 he will play 11 ... ♝g4. It's very strong. And after 11 ♝e3 he plays simply ♛c7. What can I do? Black has no weakness except the bishop on b4, but how can I use this? I should play 11 ♝e3 and after 11 ... ♛c7 something like 12 a3 ♝a5 13 e5 ♞xe5 14 ♞xe5 dxe5 15 b4 cxb4 16 axb4 ♝b6 17 ♞c3. No, it looks like a draw. But 11 ♝e3 is the best move, of course.

60

11 ♗e3

KORCHNOI: He made this move after long thinking. Well, he has now a threat of a3 and b4. In older times, I would meet a3 by ♕a6 and, God knows! But now I am playing against the most dangerous attacking player in the world, not mentioning that he is the world champion. So I have to play more carefully.

11 ... ♕c7
12 a3 ♗a5
13 ♗f4

KORCHNOI: He could have played more slowly, some knight to d2, hoping to put it on c4 and in the long run to arrange pressure on d6 and win the pawn, but it's not in his style. He wants everything. He wants to win on the spot. My next move is the only one.

13 ... ♘e5

KASPAROV: Oh! I made a terrible mistake. I missed the chance to play e5 and open my bishop on g2. What can I do now? Playing b4 is maybe the only chance, but anyway I have losing position with the white pieces after fourteen moves. It's terrible. It's very unpleasant. I'm without pawns.

14 b4

KORCHNOI: Bishop b6 is possible, but again, just as he wants to take a partner alive,

so I want to take everything he offers me. I take the pawn.

14 ... cxb4
15 axb4 ♗xb4
16 ♕a4+ ♘7c6
17 ♘d4

KORCHNOI: Now he threatens to win the piece. To take on e5, to take on c6, then to take on b4. I have only two moves: ♗c5 or a5. After ♗c5 I don't like the move ♘b3; he takes my strong bishop. Well, God knows what's better. I play a5.

17 ... a5

KASPAROV: That strange move gives me some chances. I can play now ♘c3. Maybe he missed this move.

18 ♘c3

KORCHNOI: That's very strong, very strong. I would say I have underestimated this move. I like my bishop and I don't want to exchange it. If I take on c3, ♘b5 and ♘xc3. No. I believe it is best if I develop myself and all tactical tricks do not work for him.

18 ... ♗d7

KASPAROV: After the mistake a5, that's a very good move, because it's Black's only chance to keep his bishop on b4. What can I do now? Maybe try to arrange some demonstration on the kingside with ♘d5, ♘f5 and ♕d1 and try to push my pawns. No, it should be losing anyway. It's terrible. It's no use to think a lot in this position.

19	♘d5	♛d8
20	♘f5	0-0
21	♕d1	♝c5
22	♖c1	a4
23	g4	

KORCHNOI: That's typical of Kasparov. I go. I have my trump.

| 23 | ... | a3 |
| 24 | g5 | |

KORCHNOI: Knight f6? Knight h6? To hell with it! a2.

| 24 | ... | a2 |

KASPAROV: I should play 25 ♕h5. Maybe some threats with ♘f6. If he plays 25 ... ♘d3 maybe 26 ♘f6 gxf6 27 ♕h6 ♝xf5 28 gxf6. Okay it's a chance in *Zeitnot*. He has just five minutes. Maybe it's my chance.

25	♕h5	♝xf5
26	exf5	♝d4
27	♝xe5	♘xe5
28	♝e4	♖e8
29	♖c7	a1♕

KASPAROV: Okay, I should take this queen. Of course there's a good chance that Korchnoi is nervous. He asked the referee for a new queen. That's not necessary in *Zeitnot*. Maybe there is a chance now; he has ten moves in maybe a minute.

| 30 | ♖xa1 | |

KORCHNOI: Oh thank you. I take it.

| 30 | ... | ♖xa1 + |
| 31 | ♔g2 | ♖a2 |

KASPAROV: Now the only chance is a very unusual move. ♘e7 and f6, that's nothing. Only 32 ♖e7. He couldn't have expected it. This is a chance. Okay, he won't like this move.

| 32 | ♖e7 | |

KORCHNOI: I think ♘g6 wins. ♘g6 wins! No. What is he threatening? I don't understand. I take it. I have one more move in time trouble.

| 32 | ... | ♖xf2 + |
| 33 | ♔g3 | ♖xe7 |

KASPAROV: What is he doing? He takes on e7. This is my only chance. Now he has two extra rooks and two pawns, but I have a threat of mate in two moves. This is my chance.

| 34 | f6 | ♘g6 |

KASPAROV: Okay, take on e7. Hey, maybe it's really a draw. Or maybe I give him mate. Who knows?

| 35 | ♘xe7 + | |

KORCHNOI: Can I take on e7? God knows what's better. I can't calculate it, but it looks dangerous. I go away.

| 35 | ... | ♔f8 |

KASPAROV: Unfortunately he missed 35 ... ♘xe7 36 fxe7 and I could even win the position. Now I take on h7, 36 ♕xh7 and if he plays 36

62

... ♘e7 it's mate in five moves: ♕h8+, ♕xg7+, ♕xg8+, ♕xf7+ and ♕xb7 mate. Fantastic. Maybe I'm winning.

36 ♕xh7

KORCHNOI: Now mate in one is threatened. I have to destroy everything. I take it.

36 ... ♗xf6

KASPAROV: Oh no. I can't win this game. Maybe take on g6. Of course, I should take on g6 and take his rook. Maybe it's a chance.

37	♘xg6+	fg
38	♔xf2	♕b6+
39	♔g2	♕b2+
40	♔h3	♗xg5
41	♕xg6	♕f6
42	♕xf6+	

½:½

Kasparov and Korchnoi analysing their game to a fascinated gallery.

63

GAME SIX
PORTISCH-NUNN

1 d4 ♘f6 2 ♘f3 g6 3 c4 ♗g7 4 g3 0-0 5 ♗g2
c6 6 ♘c3 d5 7 cxd5 cxd5 8 ♘e5 e6 9 0-0
♘fd7 10 f4 ♘xe5 11 dxe5 ♕b6+ 12 ♔h1
♘c6 13 b3 ♗d7 14 ♘a4 ♕b5 15 ♗a3 ♖fd8
16 ♕d2 b6 17 ♘c3 ♕a5 18 ♗b2 ♖ac8
19 ♖fd1 ♗e8 20 ♖ac1 ♗f8 21 a3 ½:½

GAME SIX

PORTISCH - NUNN

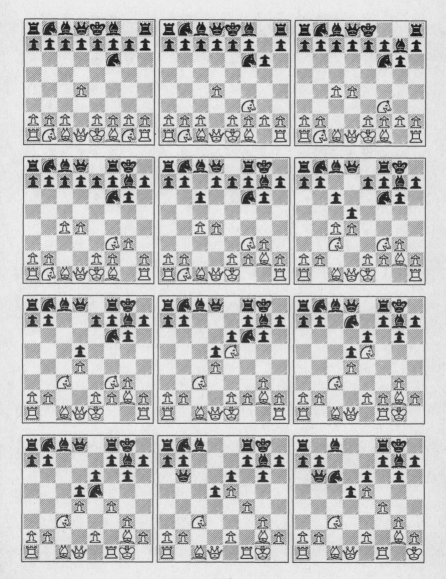

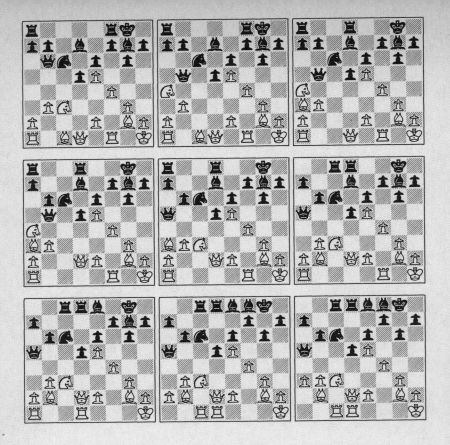

$1/2 : 1/2$

66

Portisch - Nunn

1	d4	♘f6
2	♘f3	g6
3	c4	♗g7
4	g3	0-0
5	♗g2	

The solid fianchetto is one of Portisch's favourite systems against the King's Indian.

5 ... c6

Rather than play 5 ... d6, leading to a normal King's Indian, Nunn opts for a more solid continuation. Black prepares a stake out in the centre with d7-d5.

6	♘c3	d5
7	cxd5	cxd5
8	♘e5	

Uncovering the fianchettoed Bishop and hoping for pressure against the Black pawns.

8	...	e6
9	0-0	♘fd7

Popularised by Kasparov as an equalising weapon against Karpov, so now everybody's playing it. On the other hand 9 ... ♘fd7 leads to a rather tedious position which doesn't really suit John Nunn. Look at his game against Kasparov later on. 9 ... ♘bd7 is no good, eg. 10 ♗f4 ♘h5 11 ♘xd7 ♗xd7 12 ♗g5 h6 13 ♗e3 and White stands better with somewhat more space.

10 f4

Familiar from Game 13 of the last Kasparov-Karpov match. A less dynamic approach is 10 ♘f3 after which 10 ... ♘c6 11 ♗f4 ♘f6 12 ♘e5 ♗d7 13 ♕d2 ♘xe5 14 ♗xe5 ♗c6 gives Black an easier path to equality, Karpov-Kasparov (3) London-Leningrad 1986.

10 ... ♘xe5

Well, Kasparov played 10 ... f6 and a typical e4 versus e5 position was reached after 11 ♘f3 ♘c6 12 ♗e3 ♘b6 13 ♗f2 f5 14 ♘e5 ♗d7 15 ♕d2 ♘c8 16 ♕e3 ♔h8! Kasparov-Karpov (11) London-Leningrad 1986. Later on Black managed to drum up some play on the kingside by means of Rg8 and g6-g5 but at this stage the chances are equal.

11 dxe5

A novelty from Portisch and a surprising one. 11 fxe5 was good for White in Vaganian-Smejkal Baden 1980, eg. 11 ... ♘c6 12 ♖f2 f6 13 exf6 ♗xf6 14 ♗e3 ♗d7 15 ♕d2 ♗d7 16 ♖af1 = −. As Kasparov did not play 10 ... ♘xe5 we must assume that he accepts this assessment.

11 ... ♕b6+
12 ♔h1 ♘c6
13 b3

The crux of White's idea. He will develop his black squared Bishop on b2 or a3, hold Black in the centre and hope for a gradual advantage on the queenside, for instance aiming for ♘c3-a4, b3-b4 and ♕d1-d2.

13 ... ♗d7

Black has nothing better

than to connect his Rooks.

14 ♘a4!

After the routine 14 ♗b2 Black can play 14 ... ♘e7! intending ♘f5-e3. White does have some advantage in space but he has to be careful.

14 ... ♕b5!

Nunn keeps control over c5.

15 ♗a3 ♖fd8

15 ... ♘b4 16 ♕d2! a5 17 ♖fc1 intending 18 ♖c5 = −

16 ♕d2 b6
17 ♘c3

Once again a difficult decision. Portisch was consuming a lot of time here trying to extract the maximum out of what is a minimal advantage and his clock is beginning to catch up with him. 17 ♖fc1 looks natural but leads to nothing after 17 ... ♖ac8 intending 18 ... ♕a5 =

17 ... ♕a5
18 ♗b2

Backwards again, but an entry with 18 ♗d6 looks premature after the surprising 18 ... ♗c8. Black threatens ♖xd6! and finds a comfortable square on a6 for his Bishop. Maybe he can also try to undermine the d6 square with f7-f6.

18 ... ♖ac8

19 ♖fd1 ♗e8
19 ... d4 20 ♘e4 = –
20 ♖ac1 ♗f8
In the post mortem, Portisch pointed out the interesting possibility 20 ... d4?! 21 ♘e4 ♕xa2 22 ♘d6

when White's pressure amply compensates for the sacrificed pawn. After struggling to reach a playable position Nunn is unwilling to give him this possibility and continues in solid style.

21 a3
½:½
So sudden, but really there is little either side can do without weakening their position. If play continued there would probably be some exchanges on the c-file.

Portisch, Martin

Lajos Portisch started the tournament with two solid draws against the English players.

MERYL EVANS '56

ROUND THREE

Game No.7	Nunn	1:0	Short
Game No.8	Korchnoi	0:1	Portisch
Game No.9	Hübner	0:1	Kasparov

The pairings for this round brought three grandmasters against their least favourite opponents. Short has a wretched score against Nunn, Korchnoi in recent years has seemed unable to play against Portisch, while Hübner has yet to open his score against the world champion. All three games continued the established trends, and all were very fine games, two producing mating finishes.

Nunn gave a model display on the white side of the Ruy Lopez, ending with a nice sacrificial combination. Kasparov produced a stunning series of mating ideas in a middle-game without queens. Korchnoi talked himself out of his game with Portisch - sometimes he seems to have too deep a grasp of the game for his own good.

All three games from this round were later featured in the BBC Chess Classic Series. At the start, seeing the formidable array of players, the worry had been that there would be too many heavyweight, dull draws. Now the production was already becoming embarrased by the number of fine games. How could the players be told that their brilliancies might not be wanted?

SCORES: Kasparov 2½, Portisch 2, Nunn,
Short & Korchnoi 1½, Hübner 0.

GAME SEVEN
NUNN-SHORT

1 e4 e5 2 ♘f3 ♘c6 3 ♗b5 a6 4 ♗a4 ♘f6 5 0-0 ♗e7 6 ♖e1 b5 7 ♗b3 d6 8 c3 0-0 9 h3 ♘a5 10 ♗c2 c5 11 d4 ♕c7 12 ♘bd2 ♘c6 13 d5 ♘d8 14 ♘f1 ♘e8 15 a4 ♖b8 16 ab ab 17 b4 c4 18 ♘g3 g6 19 ♘h2 ♗g7 20 ♖f1 ♗d7 21 f4 ♗h4 22 ♕f3 f5 23 fe de 24 ef ♗xg3 25 ♕xg3 ♘xf5 26 ♕f2 ♘b7 27 ♘g4 h5 28 ♖a6 hg 29 ♖xg6+ ♘g7 30 ♖xg7+ 1:0

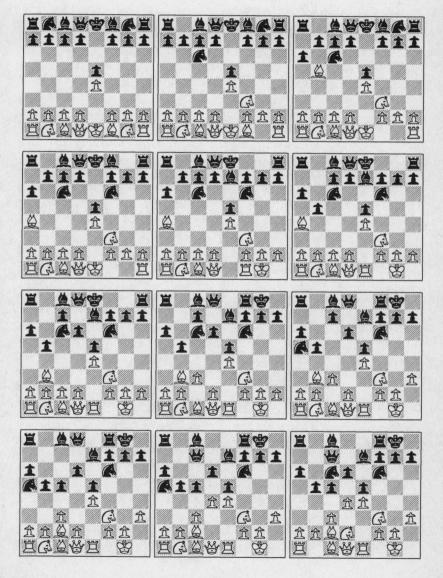

74

1:0

*After his duel with Kasparov, John Nunn
seemed more peacefully inclined this round.*

Nunn - Short

1	e4	e5
2	♘f3	♘c6
3	♗b5	a6
4	♗a4	♘f6
5	0-0	♗e7
6	♖e1	b5
7	♗b3	d6

Defending the Ruy Lopez in this closed manner has always seemed to me to be a bit masochistic. Black has a long hard fight to an equal game.

8	c3	0-0
9	h3	♘a5
10	♗c2	c5
11	d4	♕c7
12	♘bd2	♘c6

Inviting White to close the centre. Black has a host of alternatives the most popular of which is 12 ... cxd4.

13 d5

Nunn finds that this is the most logical move. 13 dxc5 hoping for later occupation of d5 doesn't lead to much after 13 ... dxc5 14 ♘f1 ♗e6 15 ♘e3 ♖ad8 and Black has other adequate plans.

13 ... ♘d8

The most flexible retreat available. Black must hang back for a while and try to arrange f7-f5 by means of ♘f6-e8 and g7-g6. His position is a tough nut to crack but it does seem rather short on counterplay. Other moves don't improve; eg:

a) 13 ... ♘a5 14 b3! ♗d7 15 ♘f1 ♗b7 16 c4 ♖fb8 17 ♘e3 ♗f8 (17 ... bxc4! Keres) 18 ♘f5 ♘d8 19 ♘h2 with an enduring initiative - Karpov-Anderssen Stockholm 1969.

b) 13 ... ♘b8 14 a4! ♗b7 1 c4 b4 16 ♘f1 ♘bd7 17 g4 + − Tseshkovsky-Henry Dresden 1969. White has successfully blocked the queenside and can now turn to his kingside attack with every chance of success.

c) 13 ... ♘a7 14 ♘f1 ♗d7 15 g4 ♘c8 16 ♘g3 + − Klovan-Schneider Jurmala 1978. Black's pieces on the queenside do not make a good impression.

It therefore seems like an attempt by Nigel Short to surprise the good Doctor. The attempt misfires.

14 ♘f1

Either 14 c4 ♗d7 15 ♗d3 g6 16 ♘f1 or 14 a4 ♖b8 15 axb5 axb5 16 b4 ♘b7 17 ♘f1 ♗d7 18 ♗e3 + = were possible but the theme is the same. White wants to close down the queenside and turn to a kingside attack.

14 ... ♘e8

A typical move in this system.

15 a4

15 g4 is also possible but an outright attack with preparation gives Black more chance to hang on, eg. 15 ... g6 16 ♘g3 ♗g7 17 ♔h2 f6 18 ♗e3 ♗d7 19 ♕d2 ♘f7 20 ♖g1 ♔h8 21 ♖af1 ♖g8 22 ♘e1 ♖af8 with a very strong defensive position.

15 ... ♖b8
16 axb5 axb5
17 b4!

17 ... c4

Nunn regards this as a mistake preferring the more flexible 17 ... g6. 17 ... c4 gives White a square on d4 for his Knight after a later f2-f4, exf4 and possibilities to penetrate on the a-file with ♗e3 and ♖a7.

Nigel feels that his position should be stable enough to weather any storm but this assessment turns out to be incorrect.

18 ♘g3

18 ♘3h2! f6 19 f4 ♘f7 20 ♘f3 g6 21 f5 ♘g7 22 g4 + − Karpov-Spassky USSR Championship 1973.

18 ... g6
19 ♘h2 ♗g7
20 ♖f1!

Prefacing an immediate f2-f4 which is met by 20 ... ♗h4! 21 ♕f3 f5! with counterplay.

20 ... ♗d7?!

20 ... f5 was right out, eg. 21 exf5 gxf5 22 ♗h6 but 20 ... f6 looks like the best defense rushing the Knight on d8 to a good square, eg. 21 f4 exf4 22 ♗xf4 ♘f7! Obviously White is better after 23 ♘f3 ♘e5 24 ♘d4 but Black's position would be superior to the game.

21 f4 ♗h4
22 ♕f3 f5

Crisis time, but with a correct sequence of captures Nunn manages to refute Black's play.

23 fxe5!

23 exf5? ♗xg3 24 ♕xg3 ♗xf5

23 ... dxe5

23 ... f4 24 ♘e2 dxe5 25 g3! ♗xg3 26 ♘xg3 ♘f7 27 ♘g4 ♗xg4 28 hxg4 fxg3 29 ♕xg3 intending ♗e3 + − with much more play for White.

24 exf5 ♗xg3

24 ... gxf5 loses to 25 ♘xf5! ♖xf5 26 ♗xf5 ♗xf5 27 g4 e4 28 ♕f4 ♕xf4 29 ♗xf4 and Short is forced into this undesirable capture.

25 ♕xg3 ♘xf5

26 ♕f2

Heading both forwards and along the diagonal to a7. The communication in White's position is most impressive and there is an immediate threat of 27 g4.

26 ... ♘b7

Intending ♘d4.

27 ♘g4

The storm warning signs are posted for the black King.

27 ... h5

27 ... ♕d6 was an alternative but then White comes round the angles with the swoop 28 ♕a7! (intending 29 ♖a6) and if now 28 ... ♕xd5 then 29 ♕xb8. After 28 ♕a7 White is now in a position to threaten the strong move 29 ♖a6!

28 ♖a6!

Black's King is about to be stripped of cover.

28 ... hxg4

28 ... ♔h7 29 ♘f6+ ♔g7 30 ♘xh5+!! gxh5 31 ♗h6+! ♔h8 32 ♗xf8 ♖xf8 33 g4 + −.

29 ♖xg6+ ♘g7

30 ♖xg7+ 1:0

If ♔xg7 31 ♗h6 mates in two.

78

— The Players TV commentaries

1	e4	e5	
2	♘f3	♘c6	
3	♗b5	a6	
4	♗a4	♘f6	
5	0-0	♗e7	
6	♖e1	b5	
7	♗b3	d6	
8	c3	0-0	
9	h3	♘a5	
10	♗c2	c5	
11	d4	♕c7	
12	♘bd2		

SHORT: My biggest problem with my opening preparation in this game was that I didn't do any. The good reason for this is that John and I decided to save ourselves lugging heavy suitcases around and so we only took half the books each and we do our opening preparation together. Now unfortunately all the books are in John's room. I'm sure he's been preparing away quite merrily there. So I think I'll play something a little unusual.

12	...	♘c6
13	d5	♘d8

NUNN: Well that knight doesn't appear to have many good moves, but later it might manoeuvre its way to the kingside. For example Black might play ♘e8, then g6 and f6 and ♘g7 and ♘f7

with a sort of doubled knights on the kingside. I think my main area of attack must be on the kingside, but I'd also like to seize control of the a-file if I can, being a rather greedy person. I could do that by playing a4 immediately. But I don't suppose it makes very much difference whether I play a4 now or next move. I'll keep my options open and play ♘f1.

14	♘f1	♘e8
15	a4	♖b8
16	axb5	axb5

NUNN: I could play ♘g3, just furthering my ambitions on the kingside, but I wonder if it might be a good idea to try and stabilise the position on the queenside. If things are going to happen mainly on the kingside, I think it would be in my favour to have a closed positon on the queenside. I might be able to do this by playing b4 here. Then he'll have to worry about the possibility of my taking on c5. Sooner or later he'll probably have to play c4, then we'll get a blocked pawn structure on the queenside which is what I want.

17 b4

SHORT: That's a shame. I know John doesn't have very much experience with these types of positions, but he's playing it very sensibly. I have a slight dilemma at the moment, whether to allow him at some point to take on c5 or just to close the position immediately. I'm feeling slightly lazy today, so I don't want to have to think about bxc5 in all positons, so I'll just close it with c4.

17 ... c4

NUNN: Oh that was easy. He went c4 without me really threatening to take on c5. Now I've got an optimum position on the queenside: the a-file's open, I control it, and also the e3-a7 diagonal is opened so in some positions I might be able to support my rook going down to a7. Anyway I want to get going on the kingside now, so I'll continue my little knight tour.

18 ♘g3 g6
19 ♘h2

SHORT: Well obviously he's intending f4 at some moment. But this doesn't seem like such a worry immediately because if I continue normally with 19 ... ♘g7 then if 20 f4 I have a very annoying move 20 ... ♗h4 pinning his knight on g3. Then if he defends with

21 ♕f3, I think 21 ... f5 is very unpleasant for White because suddenly his pieces become tactical weaknesses. So I'm quite happy so far.

19 ... ♘g7

NUNN: 20 f4 seems the logical move, but he can play 20 ... ♗h4 which is slightly annoying because my knight will be pinned for a couple of moves. It might be okay for me, but I really don't want to bother to work it out. In any case I can just play a preparatory move because Black has no threat at the moment. So I'll get my rook off its present square which allows this nasty pin.

20 ♖f1

SHORT: Hmm, I didn't consider this move properly. Somehow, I've been hoping for a mistake from John, but he doesn't seem to have made any yet. Now what am I supposed to do here? I don't like the look of 20 ... f5 at all, he simply takes 21 exf5 and if 21 ... gxf5 then 22 ♗h6 is slightly awkward. So what to do? I can play 20 ... h5, and then if 21 f4, h4, but it looks terribly weakening. I have a strong temptation to develop this knight on d8, simply playing 20 ... f6, but then 21 f4 is coming, and if I take 21 ... exf4, he simply recaptures and White has all the play. His knight is coming to f3 and d4. I don't like this. I'm in a very passive position. Maybe I shouldn't have been in such a hurry to play this move c4. It has rather reduced my options on the queenside. Anyway, it's too late for that. I'd like at some moment to be able to challenge the a-file by playing ♖a8, but I've got so many pieces on the back rank. I'll try and prepare it with ♗d7, but I'm still very passive.

```
20  ...        ♗d7
21  f4         ♘h4
22  ♕f3        f5
```

NUNN: Now it becomes sharp; I've got to start calculating concrete variations. Let's suppose somehow that these pawns are all exchanged in the centre and that he keeps recapturing with pawns whereever possible. I'll worry about the order later. Then in the resulting position, the pawns on e4, f4, d6 and g6 have gone. Then I've got a combination: I can play ♘xf5, then if he plays ♘xf5, I've got ♕g4+, or if he plays ♗xf5, I've got g4, or if he plays ♖xf5, then I've got ♗xf5, ♗xf5, g4, only move - else mate on f8 - ♕f4. Then if he exchanges queens, both the f4 bishop and rook on b8 are hanging.

So how should I make these exchanges? Well, if I play 23 exf5, he can take on g3, then play ♗xf5 which stops me taking on e5. So I should make the other capture first.

```
23  fxe5       dxe5
24  exf5
```

SHORT: This is very uncomfortable. I'm starting to miss things left, right and centre here. I'd like to play 24 ... ♗xg3 25 ♕xg3 ♗xf5 which is the positional approach, but unfortunately, this allows 26 ♘g4 and then the undefended state of my rook on f8 becomes a major importance. I can't take on c2 because of ♘h6+ and ♖xf8 mate. I really don't like this position. Well, if I take on g3 and play ♘xf5, it looks horrible without my dark squared bishop. I'm incredibly weak, but at least I have some activity. Okay I'll try:

```
24  ...        ♗xg3
25  ♕xg3       ♘xf5
26  ♕f2
```

SHORT: I thought that move was a mistake. He has some ideas with ♕c5 and ♖a7 maybe at some moment, but now I can develop my problem child with a concrete threat. If I play 26 ... ♘b7 this rules out possibilities of ♖a7 or ♕c5, and I have a counterthreat of ♘d4 hitting his queen on f2. I don't know what he is planning. I think his move's a mistake.

26 ...   ♘b7

NUNN: The move I'd really like to play here is 27 ♘g4 because it means I can answer his threat of 27 ... ♘d4 with 28 ♘f6+. After 27 ♘g4 I have all sorts of threats: ♗g5 for example or ♖a6 perhaps. But now I see that after 27 ♘g4 perhaps he's intending to play 27 ... h5. That could be a bit awkward, because if the knight moves again he's got ♘d4. But, one moment, after 27 ♘g4 h5 I've got 28 ♖a6. That's a really lovely move. If he takes the knight, well it must be mate, and on the other hand, if he blocks the sixth rank by playing ♘7d6 then my own knight can take the pawn on e5. Yes, that looks really crushing, all my pieces would be cooperating in an attack against his king.

27 ♘g4

SHORT: What the hell is he doing here? I just play 27 ... h5, then 28 ♘e3 ♘d4. What's he doing. I don't understand. Surely he should have played ♘f3, but even then I had some chances. Well, I'll play it quickly.

27 ...   h5

NUNN: Now is 28 ♖a6 really as strong as I think? If he takes the knight then 29 ♖xg6+ ♘g7 is forced, 30 ♖xg7+ ♔xg7 31 ♗h6+ then if 31 ... ♔xh6 32 ♕h4+ and ♕h7 mate. Yes, this looks really crushing.

28 ♖a6

SHORT: My goodness, where did that come from. Oh that's stupid. I simply overlooked this move. If I take on g4 then ♖xg6 leads to a forced mate. Well what can I do. If 28 ... ♘bd6 then 29 ♘xe5. If 28 ... ♔g7 then he can play 29 ♗h6+. Well, I suppose it's not so surprising. All his pieces are aimed at my king. This is clearly lost. Well, let's take a piece and pray.

28 ...   hxg4
29 ♖xg6+   ♘g7
30 ♖xg7+

SHORT: It looks like the end. My only question is where I went wrong in this game. It's not entirely obvious to me. If 17 ... c4 really was the decisive mistake, it's a very difficult position for Black. Anyway time to give up.

1:0

82

GAME EIGHT

KORCHNOI - PORTISCH

1 ♘f3 c5 2 b3 ♘f6 3 ♗b2 e6 4 e3 ♗e7 5 d4 cd 6 ed 0-0 7 ♘bd2 b6 8 ♗d3 ♗b7 9 a3 d6 10 0-0 ♘bd7 11 ♖e1 ♖e8 12 c4 ♗f8 13 ♗c2 ♖c8 14 b4 g6 15 ♗a4 ♘c6 16 ♗xc6 ♖xc6 17 ♕b3 ♕c7 18 ♖ac1 ♕a8 19 ♕d3 ♗h6 20 ♖c3 e5 21 de de 22 ♕e2 e4 23 ♘d4 ♗e5 24 ♖h3 ♗g7 25 ♘4b3 ♘d3 26 ♗xf6 ♘f4 27 ♕e3 ♘xh3+ 28 gh ♗xf6 29 ♘xe4 ♕g7 30 ♘bd2 ♖d7 31 ♕f3 ♕d8 32 ♘f1 ♗d4 33 ♘e3 ♖de7 34 ♘d5 f5 35 ♘xe7 ♖xe7 36 ♕g2 ♖xe4 37 ♖xe4 fe 38 ♕xe4 ♕g5+ 39 ♔f1 ♕e5 40 ♕b7+ ♔h6 41 ♕xa7 ♕f4 42 ♔e2 ♕f2+ 0:1

GAME EIGHT
KORCHNOI - PORTISCH

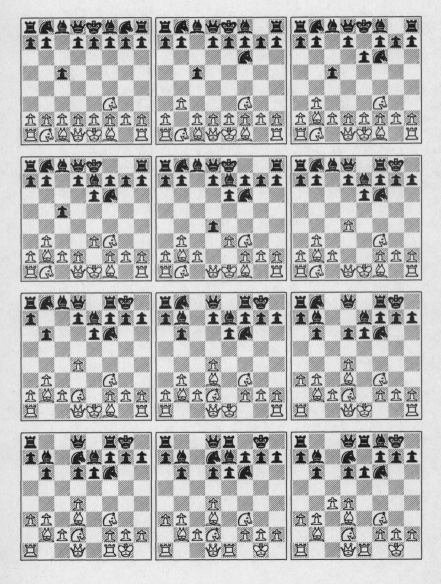

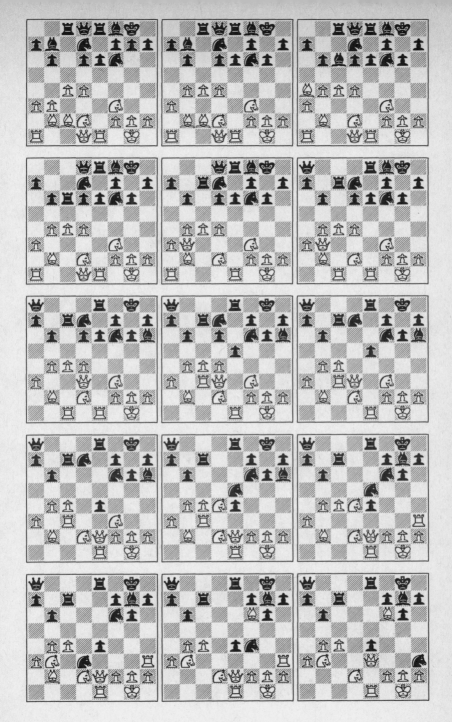

85

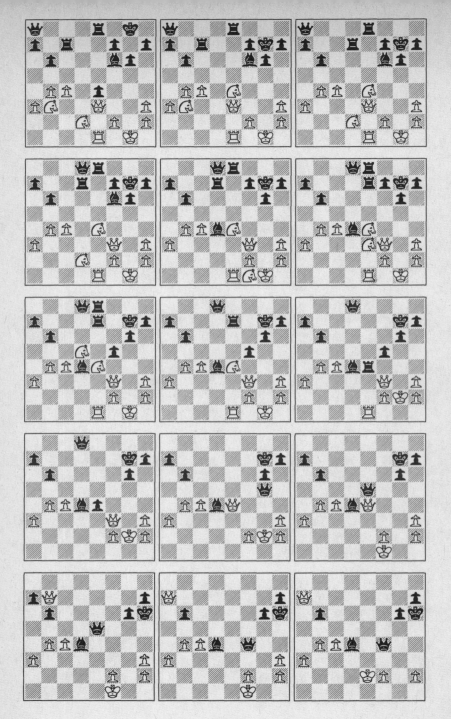

Korchnoi - Portisch

1	♘f3	c5
2	b3	♘f6

Black could play to blot out White's fianchetto with 2 ... d6, intending 3 ... e5. In that event Korchnoi would probably have delayed ♗c1-b2 waiting for Black to declare his intentions. g2-g3 and ♗f1-g2 would be one way to do this.

3	♗b2	e6
4	e3	♗e7
5	d4	cxd4
6	exd4	0-0
7	♘bd2	b6
8	♗d3	♗b7
9	a3	d6
10	0-0	♘bd7

We have transposed to a variation of the 4 e3 Queen's Indian and it's a position which doesn't really confer much advantage to White. It's difficult to do without c2-c4 and when White plays this move, Black will always have the opportunity for counterplay against these central pawns. Incidentally the two players have contested this position before in Linares 1985 — these private duels are often a feature between two old rivals.

| 11 | ♖e1 | ♖e8 |
| 12 | c4 | ♗f8 |

To be followed by g6 and ♗g7

| 13 | ♗c2 | |

Trying to force Black into modifying his plan. White intends b3-b4 and ♗a4, pinning the Knight on d7. As usual with these hedgehog-like positions Portisch has enough resources to keep a balance.

| 13 | ... | ♖c8 |
| 14 | b4 | g6 |

14 ... ♕c7 was a decent alternative.

15	♗a4	♗c6
16	♗xc6	♖xc6
17	♕b3	♖c7

Avoiding a possible advance with 18 d5! White now has to be more patient.

| 18 | ♖ac1 | |

Korchnoi must have been contemplating 18 a4! at

this point and this advance of the queenside pawns looks quite good for White. A further 19 b5 and eventually 6 a4-a5 is on the menu. Maybe he was trying to lure an off-form Portisch into time trouble with outwardly quiet moves, saving any clarification until later on.

18 ...   ♛a8!

19 ♛d3

Intending ♞e4

19 ...   ♝h6!

Excellent unstereotyped play. With less space Portisch challenges Korchnoi with a pin on the ♞d2.

20 ♜c3?

20 ♜c2 was no better when 20 ... ♜ec8 21 ♞b3 a5! is more than adequate for Black but 20 h4!, intending 21 ♞g5 and 22 ♞de4 was a good plan.

20 ...   e5!

So many exclamation marks but Portisch is playing very fine chess. By contrast 20 ... ♜ec8 is less to the

point and less good. Black now threatens 21 ... e4.

21 dxe5

21 d5 ♜ec8! intending 22 ... b5

21 ...   dxe5

22 ♛e2

A common feature of games between these two players is that they both tend to get into time trouble. You might think that age is taking its toll but they've been doing that all their lives.

22 ...   e4

23 ♞d4   ♞e5

The logical follow up to the space gaining 22 ... e4. White now has the opportunity of sacrificing his Queen to relieve his difficult position but Portisch could not have avoided this. Korchnoi tries to defend without this resource and goes under.

24 ♜h3?

24 ♞xe4(!) ♞xe4 25 ♛xe4 ♞f3+ 26 gxf3 ♜xe4 27 ♜xe4 was the best chance.

24 ...   ♝g7

Black shouldn't take on d2 provoking trouble on the h-file.

25 ♞4b3   ♞d3!

Black's game is winning. An advanced Knight like this is worth everything in such a position.

26	♗xf6	♘f4!
27	♕e3	♘xh3+
28	gxh3	♗xf6
29	♘xe4	♔g7
30	♘bd2	
30 ♕f4 ♗e5!		
30	...	♖d7

Intending 31 ... ♖xd2!

31	♕f3	♕d8
32	♘f1	♗d4
33	♘e3	♖de7

Intending f7-f5 − +

34	♘d5?	f5!
35	♘xe7	♖xe7!

If 35 ... ♕xe7 he can play 36 ♕d1

36	♔g2	♖xe4
37	♖xe4	fxe4
38	♕xe4	

A last hope in time trouble.

38	...	♕g5+
39	♔f1	♕e5
40	♕b7+	♔h6
41	♕xa7	♕f4
42	♔e2	♕e4+

0:1

Martin, Portisch

OFF THE BOARD

As may be inferred from Kasparov's reaction to the proposal of a one o'clock start for each round, he did not find a leisurely beginning to the day entirely objectionable.

In fact, he was allowed special dispensation to breakfast at 10:15 each morning even though the hotel restaurant officially closed at 10:00. As some compensation to the restaurant staff, his requirements were highly predictable.

After a starter of cornflakes or natural yoghourt, fruit yoghourts having fallen into some disfavour after Karpov Korchnoi, Baguio City, 1978, there infallibly followed grilled fillet of steak garnished with onion and tomato salad.

-Korchnoi, by contrast, found all forms of yoghourt quite resistible. His preparation for each new day instead consisted of porridge enriched with jam. Students of such matters reported no obvious daily pattern over flavour of jam.

— The Players TV commentaries

KORCHNOI: The person I meet today is a difficult nut to crack, well for me at least. In 1983 I played in a Candidates match against him and I won effortlessly, without a fight. Since then I have lost count of how many games I have lost - five or six with one or two draws made by sheer luck... I know that he is a professor of chess, that he knows everything that he is doing, that he is very well prepared at home. Perhaps I try somehow to astonish him in every game. So, on the first move I may play d4, e4, ♞f3, c4. Well I'm stuck to the move ♞f3. I played already several games and I lost them one after the other. Well still I am inclined to play ♞f3 the first move.

1	♞f3	c5
2	b3	♞f6
3	♗b2	e6
4	e3	♗e7
5	d4	cxd4
6	exd4	0-0
7	♞bd2	b6
8	♗d3	♗b7
9	a3	d6
10	0-0	♞bd7
11	♖e1	♖e8
12	c4	♗f8
13	♗c2	♖c8

KORCHNOI: The position looks promising; White has more space and prospects to attack on the king or queenside. My last move, 13 ♗c2 was a very unusual idea, but I cannot find what to do in this position. I see well the plan of Portisch. He is developing his kingside and slowly will create threats if I do nothing. What shall I do. If one player moves ahead and the other is left standing, just being stale, then the game is over. I have to do something, so I'm pushing my pawns on the queenside.

14 b4

PORTISCH: I expected this of course, because that was the idea of 13 ♗c2. He will probably play ♗a4 next. I have many good moves now at my disposal, but which might be the best? I can play ♖c7, but that maybe loses a tempo. I can play ♛c7, but it's a bit early to decide where I should place my queen. But g6 is a good move - it belongs to the system.

14	...	g6
15	♗a4	♗c6
16	♗xc6	

PORTISCH: This a surprise. Am I worse here? Maybe I

am worse, because he has some pressure at the centre. Well, I have no choice. I have to take the bishop.

16 ...   ♖xc6
17 ♕b3   ♖c7

KORCHNOI: What shall I do now? I cannot push my pawns further on. On the other hand, if I don't push this pawn, then the pawn on c4 is doomed. It will be attacked by all the black pieces. The only way for me to defend it would be to double rooks on the c-line. Then he will play ♗h6 and pin my knight and eventually take it, then he will double or triple his heavy pieces on the c-line. Sooner or later he will play e5, b5, a5, and all my pawns will collapse. All the pride of my position, my pawns on the queenside will be taken away.

What shall I do? Maybe my last move was wrong, maybe I had to play ♕a4, hoping to attack a7 eventually. Well, I am thinking too long. If I don't find a plan this game is over. How is this? It looks ridiculous. The position looks full of life, yet I believe that it is dead lost. So awkward a position. I don't know. I am doomed like all the previous games, I cannot do anything against him.

So, the position is lost.

Well, let's play a few moves. I do not resign in this position.

18 ♖ac1

PORTISCH: That's not what I was afraid of. I was much more afraid of pushing the pawns on the queenside, b5 or a4. Oh, I think I'm all right. Still, if he offers me a draw perhaps I would accept, but Korchnoi never offers a draw. I don't offer either, so I just play.

Where should I play the queen, b8 or a8? I think a8 is better because it's controlling the long diagonal. Perhaps I have some pressure on e4 and d5.

18 ...   ♕a8
19 ♕d3   ♗h6

KORCHNOI: This I hadn't expected. It is in the plan of Black, but a bit too early. Okay, I want to move my knight from d2 to b3 and play c5. In that case, when I play c5, tactically the knight on f6 would be exposed to the bishop on b2. So I have a chance to do it.

20 ♖c3

PORTISCH: Is that really a good move? Why did he close the diagonal of his bishop? I can double rooks on the c-line, but I have an even stronger move. What about e5? Yes, e5 works because the diagonal is blocked. I'm even threatening e4. So now I really have chances. He's very pressed for time, so let's start to make complications. 20 ... e5 is a good move.

20 ... e5

KORCHNOI: Ehh, I made a mistake. I made a mistake. I just had in view that the bishop on b2 will attack the knight on f6, and then I closed the bishop's diagonal. Now ... e4 is threatening and I cannot move my queen; after ... e4 the knight on f3 has no square to go to. Well now I have to play d5 or to take on e5. If I play d5 then sooner or later he will play b5 and win the pawn on d5, then the pawn on b5 and my position will collapse. Well, perhaps I have some tactical chances after taking on e5.

21 dxe5 dxe5
22 ♛e2 e4
23 ♞d4 ♞e5
24 ♖h3

PORTISCH: This is a nice trick. Of course I won't take the knight at d2, then take on c4 because I might get into a mating attack with ♛h6 and ♞f5 if I try to win the bishop on b2. But 24 ... ♝g7 is a good move anyway, because if he takes at e4, I win the queen: 25 ♞xe4 ♞xe4 26 ♛xe4 ♞f3+. Maybe it still offers him some chance for resistance, but it is very pleasant for me to play. If after 24 ... ♝g7 he

plays 25 ♞b5, I simply play 25 ... ♖d7. Still he cannot take the pawn.

24 ... ♝g7

KORCHNOI: So he is playing in his usual solid way. Now ... ♞d3 is threatening, he attacks the rook on e1 and bishop on b2. Against this threat I have 25 ♞b5, attacking the rook, and then 26 ♝xe5. Well, temporarily it prevents his threats, but what later? I do not know. But what else? If I play 25 ♞b3, he plays 25 ... ♞d3, I take on f6, he takes with the bishop, I take ♖xd3 and he cannot take on d3 because I take on e8. Well, 25 ♞b5 doesn't give me counterplay. The knight on b5 is like a solitary stranger. No, ♞b3 is the last chance.

25 ♞4b3

PORTISCH: My opponent has very little time now. This is probably a blunder. Let's control it; Why is it a blunder? Probably he overlooked something with 25 ... ♞d3. That's a logical move. His plan, of course, is to take on f6 and I cannot take back because ♖xd3 and I'm pinned along the e-line. But I have *Zwischenzug* ♞f4. That move is winning.

25 ... ♞d3
26 ♝xf6 ♞f4

KORCHNOI: Bloody hell, I overlooked it. Well, to

resign? Well, as a player in time trouble I have a right to play a little longer, even in a hopeless position.

27	♕e3	♘xh3+
28	gh	♗xf6
29	♘xe4	♔g7
30	♘bd2	♖d7
31	♕f3	♕d8
32	♘f1	♗d4
33	♘e3	♖de7
34	♘d5	f5
35	♘xe7	♖xe7
36	♔g2	♖xe4
37	♖xe4	fe
38	♕xe4	♕g5+
39	♔f1	♕e5
40	♕b7+	♔h6
41	♕xa7	♕f4
42	♔e2	♕f2+
0:1		

Tournament veteran Viktor Korchnoi was destined to do well at OHRA.

93

GAME NINE

HÜBNER-KASPAROV

1 d4 ♘f6 2 c4 g6 3 ♘c3 d5 4 ♘f3 ♗g7
5 ♕a4+ ♗d7 6 ♕b3 dc 7 ♕xc4 0-0 8 e4 b5
9 ♕b3 c5 10 e5 ♘g4 11 ♗xb5 cd 12 ♘xd4
♗xb5 13 ♘dxb5 a6 14 ♘a3 ♕d4 15 ♕c2
♘c6 16 ♕e2 ♕xe5 17 ♕xe5 ♘gxe5 18 0-0
♘d3 19 ♖b1 ♖ab8 20 ♖d1 ♖fd8 21 ♔f1 f5
22 ♔e2 ♘ce5 23 ♘a4 ♖d6 24 ♗e3 f4 25
♗c5 f3+ 26 gf ♘f4+ 27 ♔e3 ♖f6 28 ♗xe7
♘g2+ 29 ♔e2 ♖xf3 30 ♗d6 ♘f4+ 31 ♔f1
♘g4 32 ♖d2 ♖e8 33 ♘c4 ♘xh2+ 34 ♔g1
♘g4 35 ♖f1 ♗d4 36 ♗c5 ♖g3+ 37 ♔h1
♖h3+ 38 ♔g1 ♘h2 0:1

GAME NINE

HÜBNER-KASPAROV

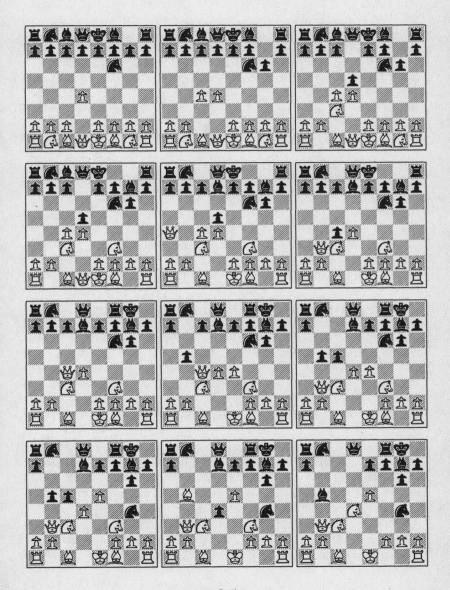

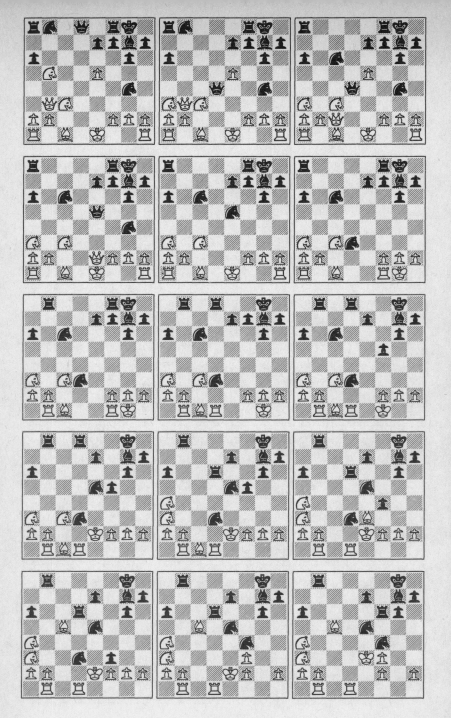

96

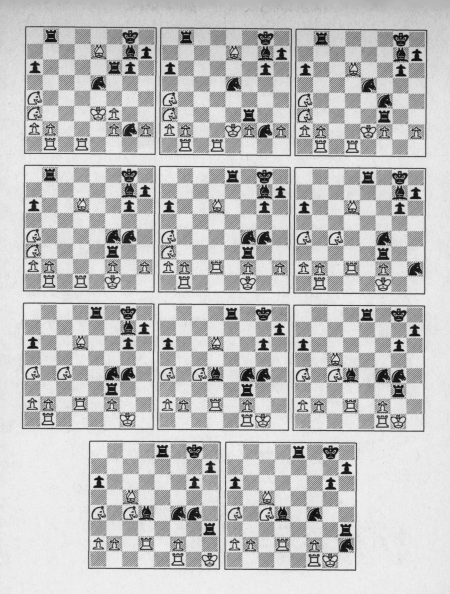

0:1

Hübner - Kasparov

1	d4	♘f6
2	c4	g6
3	♘c3	d5
4	♘f3	♗g7
5	♕a4+	

Sometimes used as a transpositional trick into the Smyslov Variation without allowing Black some of his more aggressive possibilities.

5	...	♗d7
6	♕b3	dxc4!

Strongest. 6 ... ♗c6 is recommended but I think that White has several ways to get a slight advantage after this move; 7 ♘e5 or 7 ♗f4 to name but two.

7	♕xc4	0-0
8	e4	

Hübner smells the Smyslov variation approaching. He is in for a rude shock.

8	...	b5!

A strong idea. Kasparov's thirst for activity was insatiable in Brussels. Now 9 ♘xb5 ♘xe4 10 ♘xc7 ♘c6! 11 ♘xa8 ♕a5+! is very risky and Hübner is forced to retreat leaving the initiative firmly with Black.

9	♕b3	c5!

A necessary compliment to the last move. Black must not relax for one second lest White plays ♗e3 and ♖d1.

10	e5	

If 10 dxc5 Black brings a further piece into play with 10 ... ♘a6 and White is struggling, eg. 11 ♗e3 ♘g4 −+ or 11 e5 ♘g4 12 h3 ♘xe5 13 ♘xe5 ♗xe5 14 ♗e3 ♕a5.

10	...	♘g4
11	♗xb5	

Hübner must have been sweating here. Any attempt to grab material meets with disaster. eg. 11 ♕d5 cxd4! 12 ♕xa8 dxc3 12 ♕xa7 ♘c6 −+

11	...	cxd4
12	♘xd4	♗xb5

Black had a choice between this and 12 ... ♗xe5 when 13 ♘f3 ♗xc3+ 14 bxc3 ♕b6 15 ♘d4 ♗xb5 16 ♕xb5 e5 17 ♕xb6 axb6 18 ♘b5 is still advantageous for him. Kasparov prefers to keep the Queens on for a few moves, only exchanging when White's Knight is on a bad square at a3 and there is pressure against b2.

13 ♘dxb5 a6
14 ♘a3 ♛d4

Inviting White to castle, eg. 15 0-0? ♛xe5 16 g3 ♛h5 17 h4 ♘c6 − +. This is an offer Hübner has to refuse.

15 ♛c2 ♘c6
Intending ♘b4-d3
16 ♛e2 ♛xe5!

There's no objection to an exhcnage now that the White Knights are tangled up.

17 ♛xe5 ♘gxe5
18 0-0 ♘d3

Black is clearly much better but he has to find a way to improve his position; in particular to reinforce the Knight on d3 to attack the weak b2 square.

19 ♖b1 ♖ab8
20 ♖d1 ♖fd8
21 ♔f1

A critical position. Hübner is trying to unseat the Black Knight and if he can achieve this Kasparov will only have a slight advantage. Kasparov formulates a remarkable plan of switching fronts and suddenly attacking on the kingside.

21 ... f5!
22 ♔e2 ♘ce5
23 ♘a4

23 f4? ♘xc1+ − +. Possibly the only move to protect b2.

23 ... ♖d6

Stronger than 23 ... ♖bc8. Black's simple idea is to play 24 ... ♖bd8 increasing the pressure. If White now plays 23 ... ♖d6 24 f4 then 24 ... ♖d4! 25 fxe5 ♘xc1+ 26 ♖dxc1 ♖xa4 27 ♘c4 ♗xe5 keeps the heat on.

24 ♗e3
Or 24 b3 ♘b4! is strong.
24 ... f4
25 ♗c5 f3+!

A very important continuation of the attack.

Kasparov seems to have forgotten all about b2 and with Hübner's pieces looking on from the edge proceeds to rout the White King.

26 gxf3　　♘f4+
27 ♔e3

The other possibility was 27 ♔f1. Kasparov intended 27 ... ♖xd1+ 28 ♖xd1 ♘xf3 29 ♗xe7 ♘xh2+ 30 ♔g1 ♘f3+ 31 ♔f1. Initially he found it difficult to say whether this was a winning position for Black or not, but after a further 20 minutes thought came up with 31 ... h5!

There is nothing immediate now but if you compare the position of the four Knights you see why White has problems. He can attempt to defend with 32 ♗d6 but then 32 ... ♖d8 33 ♘c4 h4! 34 ♖c1 ♖xd6!! 35 ♘xd6 h3 36 ♘e4 ♘d2+!! wins. The h-pawn walks home. A further idea is 32 ♖d8+ ♖xd8 33 ♗xd8 h4 34 ♗c7 but it seems that 34 ... ♘d2+! 35 ♔e1 meets with 35 ... g5!! and 34 ... ♘d2+ 35 ♔g1 ♘d3 36 b3 ♗d4! 37 ♗b6 ♗xb6 38 ♘xb6 h3! still wins for Black.

These samples show the remarkable coordination of the two Black Knights and the h-pawn.

27 ...　　♖f6
28 ♗xe7?

A terminal mistake in this confusing position. Even so after the better 28 ♗d4 ♖f5 29 ♗xe5 ♗xe5 30 ♘c4 ♖8f8 Black is still well on top although White can fight on.

28 ...　　♘g2+
29 ♔e2　　♖xf3
30 ♗d6　　♘f4+
31 ♔f1　　♘g4

32 ♖d2

32 ♗xb8 loses to ♖xf2+ 33 ♔g1 ♖g2+ 34 ♔f1 ♘e3+ 35 ♔e1 ♖e2 mate.

32 ...　　♖e8
33 ♘c4　　♘xh2+

The simplest way. White's King is very lonely.

34 ♔g1　　♗g4
35 ♖f1　　♗d4
36 ♗c5

36 ♘c5 ♗xf2+! 37 ♖2xf2 ♖g3+ 38 ♔h1 ♘xf2+ 39 ♖xf2 ♖e1+ 40 ♔h2 ♖h3 mate.

36 ...　　♖g3+
37 ♔h1　　♖h3+
38 ♔g1　　♘h2
0:1

A brilliant game.

— Kasparov's comments for television.

1	d4	♘f6
2	c4	g6
3	♘c3	d5
4	♘f3	♗g7
5	♕a4 +	

KASPAROV: This is a surprise for me; usually Hübner has played 5 ♗g5. It's a quiet line, but maybe he saw my game against Seirawan in Dubai. I got a very good position. Now he's trying to surprise me with this move. I'm slightly worried in this position; maybe he prepares something strong against me. Before in my praxis I have played many games with the Grünfeld defence,but with usually bad results.

5	...	♗d7
6	♕b3	dxc4
7	♕xc4	0-0
8	e4	

KASPAROV: Now if I play 8 ... ♗g4 we come to the Smyslov variation, but what about 8 ... b5? As far as I know it's very good for Black. It's impossible to understand what Hübner prepared.

8	...	b5
9	♕b3	c5
10	e5	♘g4
11	♗xb5	

KASPAROV: Oh, now it's obvious that Hübner prepared nothing for this game. He has already spent a lot of time, and now he agrees to play the worse position. I can see a much better endgame for me.

11	...	cxd4
12	♘xd4	♗xb5
13	♘dxb5	a6
14	♘a3	♕d4
15	♕c2	♘c6
16	♕e2	♕xe5
17	♕xe5	♘gxe5
18	0-0	

KASPAROV: This is the critical position. Black is much better. I can push on the queenside; I have better pieces in the centre. He has bad knights in the corner, but I should find the best move. Maybe ♖b8, maybe ♖d8, but I think that ♘d3 is necessary for me anyway. It's a very good square for the knight, d3, I have good experiences with a knight on this square.

18	...	♘d3
19	♖b1	♖ab8
20	♖d1	♖fd8
21	♔f1	

KASPAROV: Of course, Hübner is trying to get rid of this knight on d3. Now I should decide the right plan for the next moves. Of course, I can push against this pawn on b2 and press on the queenside, but I'm not sure that it's enough to win. A much better idea would be to try to begin the attack on the kingside, because all the white pieces should defend the weakness on b2 and a2. First of all I should keep my knight on d3. It's very important to include one more piece in the attack. It should be my f-pawn.

21 ...   f5
22 ♔e2   ♘ce5
23 ♘a4

KASPAROV: Now I have two promising moves: ♖bc8 and ♖d6. ♖bc8 looks very good but maybe ♖d6 is stronger. There are some threats and I see a funny position after 23 ... ♖d6 24 ♘c4 ♘xc4 25 ♖xd3 ♖xd3 26 ♔xd3 ♘a3 27 ♖a1 e5, it's very unpleasant for White. Maybe White can defend the position; for example 28 ♔e2 e4 29 ♗f4, but anyway it's very difficult and I think Hübner will choose another way. It's very unpleasant to play especially in *Zeitnot*. I'll play ♖d6, and he should think a lot.

23 ...   ♖d6
24 ♗e3   f4
25 ♗c5   f3 +
26 gxf3   ♘f4 +

27 ♔e3   ♖f6

KASPAROV: This is the point of my idea. White's king is in the centre and all my pieces are moving into the attack. Maybe the best move for him now is 28 ♗d4. I would play 28 ... ♖f5 29 ♗xe5 ♗xe5 30 ♘c4 ♖bf8. It's much better for me because he has a lot of weaknesses on the kingside, a bad king in the centre, but some chances to defend. If he takes on e7 now, it should be a winning position for me.

28 ♗xe7   ♘g2 +
29 ♔e2   ♖xf3

KASPAROV: If he plays now 30 ♗d6 I can sacrifice a rook with mate. It's a funny finish if he plays ♗d6.

30 ♗d6

KASPAROV: Okay, he's played it.

30 ...   ♘f4 +
31 ♔f1   ♘g4

KASPAROV: Of course, he can't accept this rook because of 32 ♗xb8 ♖xf2 + 33 ♔g1 ♖g2 + 34 ♔f1 ♘e3 + 35 ♔e1 ♖e2 mate. His only move is 32 ♖d2 but after 32 ... ♖e8 it's a funny position. All white pieces on the queenside. All black pieces on the kingside. But it's very important that White's king is alone on f1. I should win this game with a mate combination. I don't know how, but I feel it will happen very soon.

32	♖d2	♖e8
33	♘c4	♘xh2+
34	♔g1	♘g4
35	♖f1	

KASPAROV: Okay, he played ♖f1. That's better for me because if he took on f4 it was a very simple win for me without mate. Now after 35 ... ♗d4 I think there is no defence.

| 35 | ... | ♗d4 |
| 36 | ♗c5 | |

KASPAROV: Maybe two or three years ago, I'd have chosen another way: 36 ... ♖g3+ 37 ♔h1 ♖e5. Beautiful. If he takes on g3 then ♖h5 mate; if he takes on e5 then ♖h3+, ♔g1, ♘xe5 is winning. But now I'm getting older. I've played many games against Karpov and I should choose a more practical move.

36	...	♖g3+
37	♔h1	♖h3+
38	♔g1	♘h2
0:1		

The world champion — five minutes late and the clock still running.

OFF THE BOARD

A Russian television crew visited the tournament just once and, with unerring timing, they chose just the right day to film Gary Kasparov losing to his young Western rival.

Other crews were regular attenders and some careful negotiation was needed. As always, the tournament sponsor and organisers welcome the extra publicity but to the players — trying to concentrate on their games — the cameras are an added distraction.

At OHRA, this was aggravated because the grandmaster tournament took place in a small room — there was seating room for only a couple of dozen spectators with others relegated to an overflow room — where extra lighting was needed for the television cameras.

An agreement was made whereby filming took place for only the first 10 minutes of each playing session, whereupon the players still had to spend the next 10 minutes readjusting their eyes to the sudden gloom after the television lights went out.

The agreement was threatened when star attraction Kasparov arrived late — "We thought we had negotiated 10 minutes of Kasparov", said an irate cameraman — and thereafter the world champion was good-humouredly punctual.

ROUND FOUR:

Game No.10	Short	1:0	Kasparov
Game No.11	Portisch	½:½	Hübner
Game No.12	Nunn	½:½	Korchnoi

Hübner at last opened his score; Nunn and Korchnoi threatened to become quite interesting before a repetition of moves occurred; but there was no doubt as to the game of the round.

When Kasparov had recorded his commentary to the previous game (against Hübner) Short had been sitting in the same room listening in wonder at the world champion's streams of mating variations. After Kasparov had left the room, Nigel, still open-mouthed, said: "I have to play against that monster tomorrow". And after a remarkable game, the monster was slain. It was a scrappy game, true, with the English grandmaster overlooking the loss of a piece. His compensatory counterplay was more by accident than calculation. Apparently flustered by all the curious happenings on the board, Kasparov made a rare oversight. All in all, a quite remarkable game.

SCORES: Kasparov, Short & Portisch 2½; Korchnoi & Nunn 2, Hübner ½.

GAME TEN
SHORT-KASPAROV

1 e4 c5 2 ♘f3 d6 3 d4 cd 4 ♘xd4 ♘f6 5 ♘c3 a6 6 ♗e3 e6 7 ♕d2 b5 8 f3 ♘bd7 9 g4 h6 10 0-0-0 ♗b7 11 ♗d3 ♘e5 12 ♖he1 ♖c8 13 ♔b1 ♗e7 14 h4 b4 15 ♘a4 ♕a5 16 b3 ♘fd7 17 g5 g6 18 f4 ♘xd3 19 cd hg 20 hg d5 21 f5 e5 22 ed ♕xd5 23 f6 ♗d6 24 ♘c2 a5 25 ♗a7 ♕f8 26 ♘e3 ♕e6 27 ♘c4 ♔g8 28 ♘xd6 ♕xd6 29 ♘b2 ♖c3 30 ♘c4 ♕d5 31 ♘e3 ♕e6 32 ♖c1 ♕a6 33 ♖xc3 bc 34 ♕xc3 ♕a7 35 ♕c7 ♕d4 36 ♕xb7 ♕xd3+ 37 ♘c2 ♖h2 38 ♕c8+ ♘f8 39 ♖xe5 ♖h1+ 40 ♔b2 ♕d2 41 ♖e8 ♕d6 42 ♖d8 ♕e5+ 43 ♔a3 ♔h7 44 ♖xf8 ♕d6+ 45 b4 1:0

GAME TEN

SHORT-KASPAROV

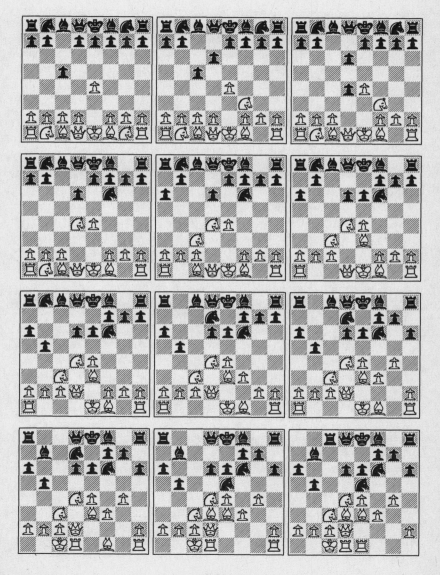

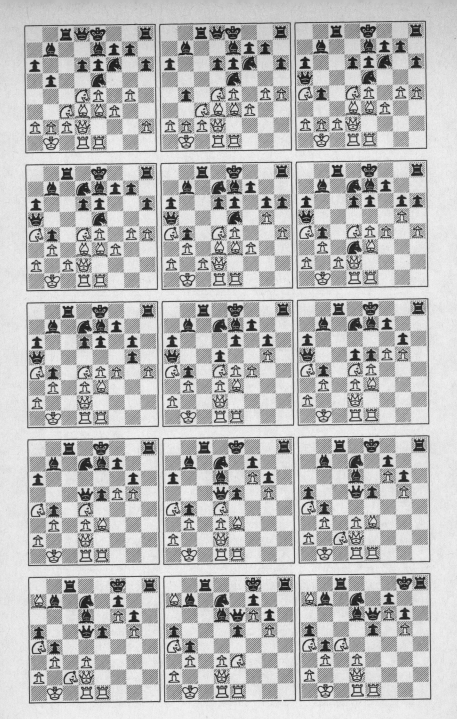

108

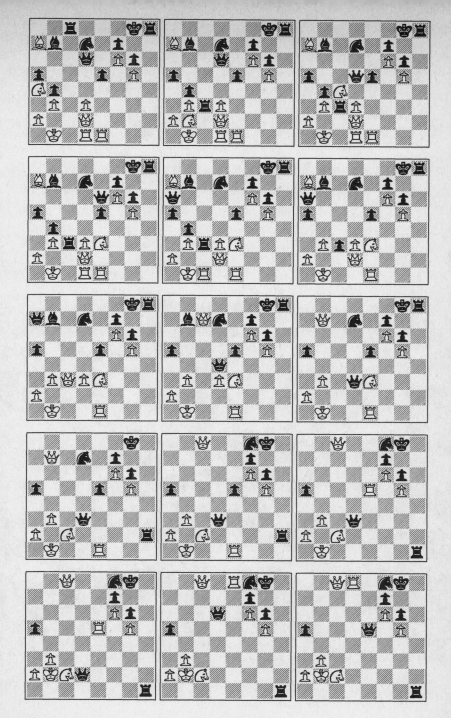

1:0

At the opening ceremony. "You'll go down
in round four", predicts Nigel Short.

Short - Kasparov

1	e4	c5
2	♘f3	d6
3	d4	cxd4
4	♘xd4	♘f6
5	♘c3	a6
6	♗e3	e6
7	♕d2	b5
8	f3	♘bd7
9	g4	h6
10	0-0-0	

A favourite variation of the English player.

10	...	♗b7
11	♗d3	♘e5
12	♖he1	

Theory gives 12 ♔b1 as best but after 12 ... b4! 13 ♘ce2 d5 the position is not at all clear.

12	...	♖c8
13	♔b1	♗e7?!

Here, Black should probably play 13 ... g5!? If then 14 h4 gxh4 15 ♖h1 ♘fd7 and Black has chances in this interesting position. At the moment the Bishop is not well placed on e7.

14	h4	b4

14 ... ♘fd7 15 g5 ♘b6 16 b3! + −

15	♘a4	♕a5

I would like to have played 15 ... d5 but 16 g5 dxe4 17 gxf6 highlights the bad position of Black's Bishop.

16	b3	♘fd7
17	g5	g6!

The best move in a difficult position. If I do not play this White threatens f3-f4 to be followed by g5-g6.

18	f4	♘xd3
19	cxd3	hxg5
20	hxg5	d5
21	f5	

I think White should have preferred 21 e5 with 22 ♖h1 to follow and sacrificial ideas of f4-f5 are in the air.

21	...	e5!
22	exd5	♕xd5

22 exd4 23 ♗xd4 intending f5-f6 + −

23	f6	♗d6

111

24 ♘c2　　a5
25 ♗a7!?

An original idea but 25 d5 might have been better, eg. 25 ... e4 26 ♗f4 intending 27 ♖h1.

25 ...　　♕f8
26 ♘e3　　♕e6
27 ♘c4　　♔g8
28 ♘xd6!?

A second strange move. Maybe 28 ♕f2! just keeping the position intact was better but after other alternatives, eg:

a) 28 ♘xa5 ♗f3 29 ♖c1 ♖xc1+ 30 ♖xc1 e4! or;

b) 28 d4 ♕f5+ 29 ♔a1 ♖xc4 30 bxc4 ♗f3 intending 31 ... e4 Black reaches a good game.

28 ...　　♕xd6

At last Black has equalized.

29 ♘b2　　♖c3
30 ♘c4　　♕d5
31 ♘e3　　♕e6?

A big mistake. Stronger was 31 ... ♕b5! intending an eventual a5-a4!

32 ♖c1　　♕a6!
33 ♖xc3!

Short finds a fine piece sacrifice but Black should still be able to draw.

33 ...　　bxc3
34 ♕xc3　　♕xa7
35 ♕c7

Now 35 ... ♘f8 looks bad in view of 36 ♘d5 with the threat of ♘e7 and Rook to the h-file. Nevertheless Black can play it, eg. 36 ... ♕d4! 37 ♘e7+ ♔h7 38 ♕xb7 ♕xd3+ 39 ♔c1 ♕c3+ with perpetual check. Note that White cannot play 37 ♗xb7? because of 37 ... ♖h2! and Black wins. Under some pressure I made a mistake.

35 ...　　♕d4
36 ♕xb7　　♕xd3+
37 ♘c2　　♖h2

It looks alright at the moment but Black's King is permanently locked up.

38 ♕c8+　　♘f8?

A final innaccuracy. 38 ... ♔h7 is the only move but even so White keeps his good position after 39 ♕c6.

39 ♖xe5　　♖h1+
40 ♔b2　　♕d2
41 ♖e8!

112

41	. . .	♛d6
42	♖d8	♛e5 +
43	♔a3	♔h7
44	♖xf8	♛d6 +
45	b4	

1:0

Notes based upon comments by Kasparov.

OFF THE BOARD

Short's win against Kasparov, reputedly the world champion's first-ever loss against a younger opponent, was still the main discussion topic.

The consensus was that this owed much to Short's having played the right move for the wrong reason — the perceived strategic justification outweighing the overlooked tactical 'refutation' — but also something to the younger man's psychological approach.

For, although Short was known readily to concede that Kasparov was still much the stronger player, he was adamant that Kasparov was far from invincible.

"There are big flaws in his game", said Nigel, as reported by the Financial Times' Dominic Lawson. "It is mainly a question of character. He is extremely egotistical".

"That is not meant to be derogatory", added Nigel. "But it means he can overestimate his position both on and off the board".

Ironically, Lawson's article cited grandmaster Raymond Keene as suggesting that similar criticisms could be levelled at Short himself who, "Sometimes makes mistakes because he cannot believe he has overlooked something". In the Kasparov game, this weakness may have rebounded to Short's advantage.

— The Players TV commentaries

1	e4	c5
2	♘f3	d6
3	d4	cxd4
4	♘xd4	♘f6
5	♘c3	a6
6	♗e3	e6
7	♕d2	b5
8	f3	♘bd7
9	g4	h6

SHORT: 9 ... h6 is rather a double-edged move in that although it temporarily holds up g5, it is a potential weakness and makes it very difficult for Black to castle kingside because h4 and g5 normally leads to a quick mate. I was looking at a few things this morning, because I expected to get something similar to this.

10	0-0-0	♗b7
11	♗d3	♘e5

KASPAROV: This is a famous theoretical position. I know that all strong English players like this position as White. There were many beatiful wins, for example Chandler-Ribli, Nunn-Ftacnik, or Short-Ftacnik, is 12 ♔b1, but after 12 ... b4 13 ♘e2 d5 it's an unclear position. It's very interesting to see what Short has prepared for this game.

SHORT: John Nunn suggested a move to me this morning, it's 12 ♖he1. I'd like to try this crazy move. Of course it serves absolutely no function whatsoever other than preventing the thematic b4 and d5. It looks very stupid, because really I would like to have my rook on the h-file. With my rook on h1, h4 and g5 makes a lot of sense. But he's looking confident and playing the moves very quickly, I'd like to surprise him, so ♖he1.

12	♖he1	♖c8
13	♔b1	

KASPAROV: This is an important position. I should find a plan for the next moves. Maybe play g5 and try to keep my knight on e5. Maybe play ♗e7, just to develop my kingside. If he then plays h4, I play ♘d7 or b4 and d5. It should be very good for me because I have a good position in the centre.

13	...	♗e7

SHORT: Well, I'm not quite sure how I should proceed, so when in doubt, push a pawn. Normally I play h4 and g5 in these lines to remove this knight from f6. I don't even want to consider complications with b4 and d5. If they're good for him, that's just my bad luck.

14 h4

KASPAROV: Now if I play 14 ... ♘fd7 15 g5 ♘b6 he can play 16 b3. It's very unpleasant for me because he keeps c4 under control and my counterplay on the queenside is nothing. What can I do? If I play b4, he plays ♘a4. It's very dangerous for me. Now I realise that I made a mistake last move. I should have played g5. My position would have been much better than now. Now he has the simple plan just to play g5, f4 and f5. Anyway, I should find a plan to defend my position. Okay, I think b4, then ♕a5, take on d3 and play d5. It's the only chance for me, but very, very dangerous. I don't see an alternative.

14	...	b4
15	♘a4	♕a5
16	b3	♘fd7

SHORT: I'm beginning to like my position. What is he doing with his king here? His king is terribly placed and all my pieces are developed. Okay, I have the immediate problem what to do with my h-pawn. I could play h5, but this is a bit wet. The move I want to play is g5. This is starting to look nice, very nice.

17	g5	g6
18	f4	♘xd3
19	cxd3	hxg5
20	hxg5	d5

SHORT: So that's his idea. I have a very tempting move here: just e5 and then his bishops are looking very stupid, especially the one on b7. If I play e5, then I'm going to have a draw in hand, because there's no way I can lose a position like this. But objectively I think my position is worth more than just playing this quiet move. I'd really like to rip his guts open with f5. If he takes with the g-pawn, I simply recapture and this is a real holocaust. I'm threatening fxe6, I'm threatening g6, there's just no way he can survive. I guess he'd have to try e5, but then I've many possibilities. Okay, let's go for the kill.

21 f5

KASPAROV: Maybe now I have some chances. I think e5 was much more dangerous for me. Now anyway I have some chances because the position is very dangerous again; maybe right now I can use my bishops and defend my king. Most important, the position is opening. Maybe it's good for me; maybe I'll get some chances in the nearest future.

| 21 | ... | e5 |

SHORT: With his king on e8 and my rook on e1, it makes sense to open up the game. If I take on d5, he is not able to take my piece on d4, because I simple recapture, hitting his rook on h8 and threatening f6 and d6.

22 exd5   ♕xd5
23 f6

KASPAROV: Now there are new dangers in the position. He's going to play ♘c2, then play d4 and open the e-line and d-line. My king is in a very bad position. But anyway, it's not so easy for him. Of course, I should play ♗d6 and try to defend against d4 by playing e4. It's worse for me and terribly dangerous position for Black, but I have the feeling it's better than two or three moves ago.

23 ...   ♗d6
24 ♘c2   a5

SHORT: The move I'd like to play here is 25 ♗g1, intending to play ♘e3 and put my knight on c4. Unfortunately he has 25 ... ♕g2 and it's getting a little bit messy if that happens. I just want to get this bishop out of the way, so I'll put it on a7. It looks like a ridiculous move, but it's not the first time I've done it in this variation.

25 ♗a7

KASPAROV: Oh this is a fantastic move. I don't understand the reason. He puts his bishop in a very bad position, losing time. Okay, now my king can escape from the centre.

25 ...♔f8
26 ♘e3   ♕e6
27 ♘c4   ♔g8

SHORT: Now I have a problem. What to do next. Perhaps my bishop isn't so well placed on a7 after all. I'd like to take 28 ♘xa5, but then he has 28 ... ♗f3 29 ♖c1 ♖a8 and this guy is very good in these tricky positions. I'd like to play simply instead, just to preserve my initiative.

28 ♘xd6   ♕xd6

KASPAROV: Okay, now I think I'm okay. The only danger is 29 d4 now, but I have a very interesting idea: 29 ... ♕f5+ 30 ♔a1 ♖xc4 31 bxc4 ♗f3 and then 32 ... e4. It's very good compensation for the exchange, because I can attack his pawns and my bishop is outside. I think my position is not better, but it's a very good position. Unfortunately I'm in *Zeitnot* now. This is a problem, but it's very strange, maybe now I have the best position I have had during this game.

29 ♘b2   ♖c3
30 ♘c4   ♕d5

SHORT: I can't help feeling I'm losing control of this

position. He's suddenly got very active and I'm not sure how I'm going to get at his king on g8. I've really lost the thread here. I don't know what I should be trying to do. Well, let's hit his queen.

31 ♘e3

KASPAROV: Now he wants to put his knight on h6. Okay I play ♕e6 and I have very interesting threat to play ♕a6 and to take his bishop.

31 ... ♕e6

SHORT: Now I have a nice possibility to open up the c-file and get my rooks into play.

32 ♖c1

KASPAROV: Okay, he played fast ♖c1. Of course he missed ♕a6. It should be very good.

32 ... ♕a6

SHORT: Oh my God, where did that come from? I just lost a piece. I just can't believe it. A piece down and after having such a good position. Oh my goodness. But hang on a second, if I take 33 ♖xc3, he takes bxc3, I take ♕xc3, he takes on a7, well I have ♕c7. It's not so easy for him here. If ♘f8, I have ♘d5. Well, it's obviously my only chance.

33 ♖xc3 bc
34 ♕xc3 ♕xa7
35 ♕c7

KASPAROV: Unfortunately, I should sacrifice my piece, because ♘f8 is very dangerous because of ♘d5. Anyway, after 35 ... ♕d4 I have a very good position. My rook is protected and I have some threats for White's king.

35 ... ♕d4

SHORT: Did he really have to do that? Well, let's not bother even to think about it. I can regain my piece. I still don't like my position, but I guess this was a bit of luck.

36 ♕xb7 ♕xd3+
37 ♘c2 ♖h2

KASPAROV: If he now plays 38 ♕c8+, I have ♘f8 and he can't take on e5 because of ♕d1+ and ♕d4+. and I take his rook. I have very good position. Maybe I'm better and now Short has the same time as I. Maybe I can even win this game. It's very good.

SHORT: Three moves to make in five minutes. I feel I ought to be able to draw this position. I can just check on c8, ♔h7, ♕c6 and I'm not sure how he strengthens his position. Maybe I'm alright after all.

38 ♕c8+ ♘f8

SHORT: What is he doing. I just really can't understand this move. He's left a pàwn *en prise*. 39 ♖xe5 ♕d1+ 40

♔b2 ♕d4+ 41 ♕c3, I'm absolutely baffled by this.

39 ♖xe5

KASPAROV: Okay, he missed the rook. Oo-ooh. This is a very unpleasant surprise. I can't play ♕d1+ and ♕d4+ because of ♕c3. He protects his rook and he as a pawn more and many threats. But I can play ♖h1+ then ♕d2, queen check on c1, then check on h3. It's a strong attack and I should be first. Okay, no time to think more.

39 ...   ♖h1+
40 ♔b2   ♕d2

SHORT: What's he doing again? I don't understand. I think the guy's gone crazy. He has one check, ♕c1+ and I move my king to c3. Then he can't play ♖h3+ because my queen is protecting this square. I think he's just cracked up here. It's very strange. Well, as he's not threatening anything, I can create a few threats of my own. 41 ♖e8, threatening ♖xf8; this leads to a forced win. It's very simple. I can hardly believe it. Well, he's slumped at the board now. I guess it must be over.

41 ♖e8

KASPAROV: Okay, this is my fault. I couldn't play during this day. I had to realise my feelings and my chess mentality and try to avoid such a complicated game today. Anyway, now there's no choice. But it's losing.

41 ...   ♕d6
42 ♖d8   ♕e5+
43 ♔a3

KASPAROV: Maybe after 43 ... ♔h7 44 ♖xf8 ♕d6+, if he plays 44 ♔a4 I play ♖h4+, then sacrifice both rook and queen and it's a stalemate. But if he plays 44 b4 ... What can I do?

43 ...   ♔h7
44 ♖xf8   ♕d6+
45 b4

KASPAROV: Okay, I should resign. No moves. Mate and no perpetual check. It's very unpleasant to lose this game, because he played with many mistakes too. But anyway, someone should make the last mistake. Very pity.

0:1

GAME ELEVEN

PORTISCH-HÜBNER

1 d4 d5 2 c4 c6 3 ♘c3 ♘f6 4 e3 e6 5 ♘f3 ♘bd7 6 ♕c2 ♗d6 7 b3 0-0 8 ♗e2 e5 9 cd ♘xd5 10 ♘xd5 cd 11 de ♘xe5 12 ♗b2 ♗b4+ 13 ♔f1 ♘xf3 14 ♗xf3 ♗e6 15 ♕d3 ♗e7 16 ♔e2 ♕a5 17 ♖hc1 ♖ac8 18 a3 h6 19 ♔f1 ♕b6 20 ♔g1 ♕d6 21 ♗d1 ♖c6 22 ♖xc6 bc 23 ♗c2 f5 24 b4 c5 25 bc ♕xc5 26 ♕d4 ♕xd4 27 ♗xd4 ♔f7 28 ♔f1 ♖c8 29 ♗d3 ♗f6 30 ♔e2 ♗xd4 31 ed ♖c3 32 ♔d2 ♖b3 33 ♗c2 ♖b6 34 ♖e1 f4 35 ♔c3 ♖c6+ 36 ♔b2 ♖c4 37 ♖d1 ♔e7 38 ♗b3 ½:½

119

GAME ELEVEN

PORTISCH - HÜBNER

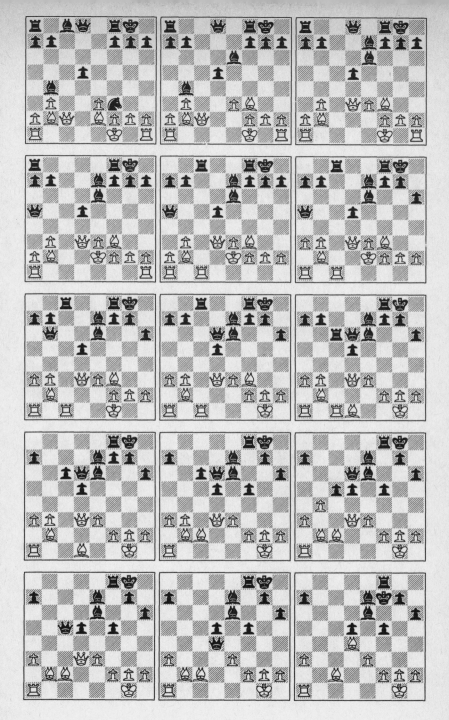

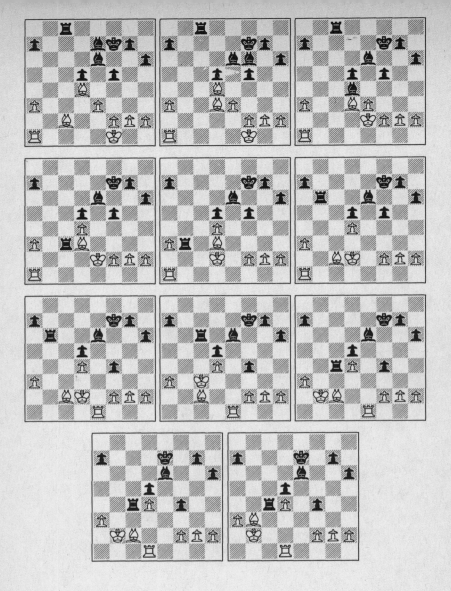

½:½

Portisch - Hübner

1	d4	d5
2	c4	c6
3	♘c3	♘f6
4	e3	e6
5	♘f3	♘bd7
6	♕c2	

Kasparov chose the more usual 6 ♗d3 in a later round versus Hübner, and the German GM reacted with 6 ... ♗b4!? instead of the usual Meran, 6 ... dxc4.

6	...	♗d6
7	b3	0-0
8	♗e2	e5

With this, Black cleans the centre and generates mass simplification, but he also limits himself to tedious equality at best.

9	cxd5	♘xd5
10	♘xd5	cxd5
11	dxe5	♘xe5
12	♗b2	♗b4+

13	♔f1	♘xf3
14	♗xf3	♗e6

Black has an IQP, while White has forfeited the right to castle. Chances are roughly level and not much happens to disturb the balance of power in subsequent events.

15	♕d3	♗e7

White threatened ♕d4.

16	♔e2	

Also possible is 16 h4 (16 ... ♗xh4? 17 g3) followed up by 17 g3 and ♔g2.

16	...	♕a5
17	♖hc1	♖ac8
18	a3	h6
19	♔f1	

19 b4 deserves consideration. Portisch plays it later after he has regrouped his KB to cover the c4 square to mete out ... ♖c4.

19	...	♕b6
20	♔g1	

If 20 ♗xd5 ♕d6 21 ♖d1 ♖fd8 22 e4 ♕xh2. White protects h2, and Hübner hastens to defend d5.

20	...	♕d6
21	♗d1	♖c6
22	♖xc6	bc
23	♗c2	f5
24	b4	c5

Speedily dissolving his

'hanging pawns' and returning to an IQP situation.

25	bxc5	♕xc5
26	♕d4	♕xd4
27	♗xd4	♔f7
28	♔f1	

If 28 ♗xa7 ♖c8 restores material equilibrium.

28	...	♖c8
29	♘d3	♗f6
30	♔e2	♗xd4
31	exd4	♖c3
32	♔d2	♖b3
33	♗c2	♖b6

Now if White is seriously going to play for a win, the time has come for 34 f4! fixing Black's pawn on f5 (as well as d5) both the same colour square as his Bishop.

Portisch isn't seriously playing for a win, or maybe

he does not believe in 34 f4 g5, getting counterplay. In any case we have the anodyne:

| 34 | ♖e1?! | f4! |

Cancelling the problem.

35	♔c3	♖c6+
36	♔b2	♖c4
37	♖d1	♔e7
38	♗b3	

½:½

GAME TWELVE
NUNN - KORCHNOI

1 e4 e6 2 d4 d5 3 ♘c3 ♝b4 4 e5 c5 5 a3
♝xc3+ 6 bxc3 ♞e7 7 ♞f3 ♝d7 8 dxc5 ♛c7
9 ♝d3 ♞bc6 10 ♝f4 ♞g6 11 ♝g3 ♛a5 12
♛d2 ♛xc5 13 h4 d4! 14 ♝xg6 hxg6 15 cxd4
♛c4 16 ♖b1 b6 17 ♛e2 ♛c3+ 18 ♛d2 ♛c4
19 ♛e2 ♛c3+ 20 ♛d2 ½:½

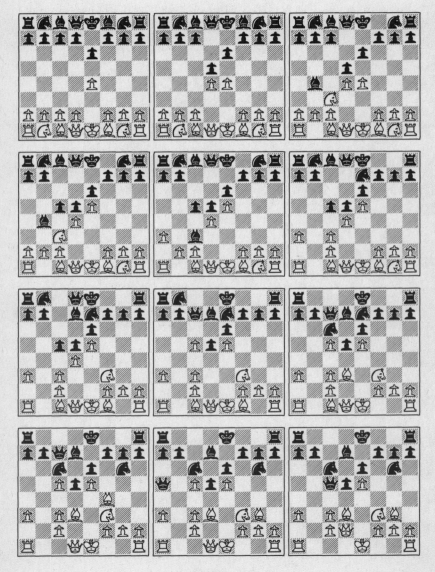

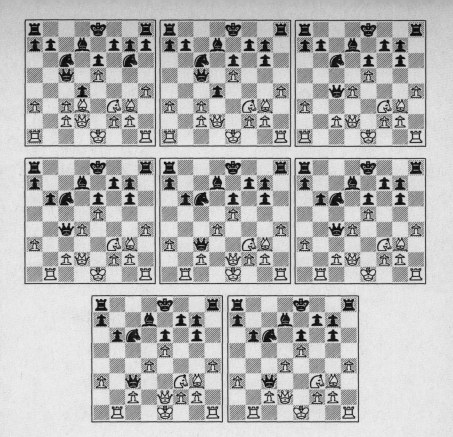

1/2:1/2

GAME TWELVE

Nunn - Korchnoi

1	e4	e6
2	d4	d5
3	♘c3	

John Nunn used to be an exponent of Tarrasch's 3 ♘d2 and won many fine games with it. However, Korchnoi invariably defends against this with 3 ... c5. This tends to lead to technical positions when White enjoys a microscopic edge.

See, for example, many games in the 1974 Karpov-Korchnoi Candidates' Final. Even in this tournament Hübner proved that it is possible to beat Korchnoi by tactical means after 3 ♘d2 c5, but that is probably too tedious a course for John Nunn's buccaneering spirit.

3	...	♗b4
4	e5	c5
5	a3	♗xc3+
6	bxc3	♘e7
7	♘f3	♗d7
8	dxc5	

This procedure was tested in the 1977/78 Spassky-Korchnoi Candidates' final. One of Spassky's ideas was to swing over the white QR for kingside attack by means of ♖b1-b4.

Of course, in exchange White must submit to the indignity of weak tripled pawns in the open c-file.

8	...	♕c7

A logical move which attacks c5 immediately and answers pressure against e5. An alternative is 8 ... ♗a4 which prevents a4 and ♗a3.

9	♗d3	

An alternative (quite logical in view of Black's omission of ... ♗a4) would be 9 a4 and if 9 ... ♕xc5 10 ♕d2 to be followed by ♗a3. Such variations were considered important during our analysis in 1977 when I was part of Korchnoi's team in the assault on the world championship. In the past ten years Korchnoi has evidently made efforts to improve Black's defensive theory.

9	...	♘bc6

Korchnoi prefers to hunt down the e5 pawn rather than reclaim c5, which would be possible after 9 ... ♕xc5 10 ♕d2 or, again, 9 ... ♗a4 to be followed by ... ♘d7 and ... ♘xc5.

10	♗f4	♘g6
11	♗g3	♕a5

A convoluted way to retrieve the pawn, but at least Korchnoi has diverted White's QB to a harmless diagonal, away from a1-f8, which would be the most dangerous for Black.

12 ♕d2   ♛xc5
13 h4

In spite of Black's ingenuity in preventing the most effective deployment of White's QB, Nunn still appears to be whipping up a promising initiative. The advance of White's h-pawn to h5 or h6 would seriously cramp Black's K-side, while 13 ... h5 destabilizes Black's Knight at g6.

Korchnoi now finds an excellent resource in the nick of time.

13 ...   d4!
14 ♗xg6

Necessary if White wants to win a pawn.

14 ...   hxg6
15 cxd4   ♛c4

At the cost of a pawn Black has stymied White's initiative, established a light square blockade and now White is prevented from castling. Nimzovitch would have approved.

16 ♖b1   b6

Black is now ready for ... 0-0-0, so Nunn bails out.

17 ♕e2   ♛c3+
18 ♕d2   ♛c4

18 ... ♛xa3 19 0-0 allows White to break the blockade and later use the open a-file.

19 ♕e2   ♛c3+
20 ♕d2

Drawn by repetition of position.

ROUND FIVE:

Game No. 13	Korchnoi	½:½	Short
Game No. 14	Hübner	1:0	Nunn
Game No. 15	Kasparov	1:0	Portisch

Korchnoi and Short both spent a good deal of thinking time rediscovering moves which had been played in one of the Kasparov-Karpov games. The world champion was grinning when he told them of this after the game. Meanwhile, Kasparov himself was producing an impressive performance against Portisch. A startling opening innovation - offering a piece in a well-known position - was followed by a still more remarkable middlegame idea. Kasparov's plan, almost unbelievably, was to increase his pressure on the centre by playing 14 a4 and 15 ♘h4. The way White's pieces bounced off the edges to find their way back to the centre looked quite magical.

Hübner's convincing win showed that his initial three losses had not disconcerted him too much.

SCORES: Kasparov 3½; Short 3; Korchnoi & Portisch 2½; Nunn 2; Hübner 1½

GAME THIRTEEN
KORCHNOI - SHORT

1 d4 ♘f6 2 c4 e6 3 ♘f3 d5 4 ♘c3 ♗e7 5 ♗g5 h6 6 ♗h4 0-0 7 ♖c1!? dxc4 8 e3 c5 9 ♗xc4 cxd4 10 ♘xd4 ♗d7 11 0-0 ♘c6 12 ♘b3 ♖c8 13 ♗e2 ♘d5 14 ♗xe7 ♘cxe7 15 ♘xd5 ♘xd5 16 ♖xc8 ♕xc8 17 ♕d4 b6! 18 ♖c1 ♕b8 19 e4 ♘f4 20 ♗f1 ♖d8 ½:½

GAME THIRTEEN

KORCHNOI · SHORT

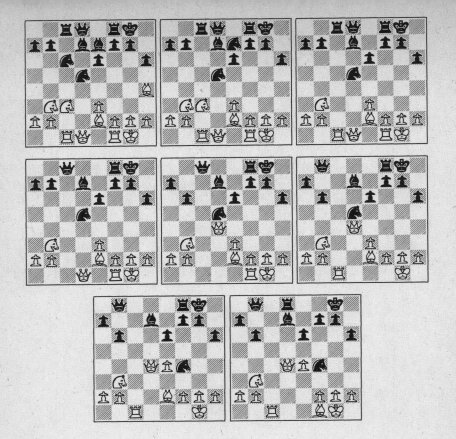

½:½

Korchnoi - Short

1 d4

In general, Short has found it more difficult to defend against 1 d4. At OHRA, England's top-rated Grandmaster sought security in the Queen's Gambit Declined, basically modelled on Karpov's defensive repertoire.

1 ... ♘f6
2 c4 e6
3 ♘f3 d5

In the 1985 Candidates' Tournament at Montpellier Short tended to play 3 ... b6 here (the Queen's Indian) not, on the whole, with encouraging results.

4 ♘c3 ♗e7
5 ♗g5 h6
6 ♗h4

Korchnoi should probably take a leaf from Kasparov's book here and exchange immediately on f6. I acted as Korchnoi's second in his 1977-78 Candidates' Final v Spassky, and his 1978 World title clash with Karpov. At that time we devoted a tremendous amount of time and energy towards finding an effective antidote to the Tartakower-Makogonov-Bondarevsky defence: 6 ♗h4 0-0 7 e3 b6 etc ...

This search was more or less fruitless and the TMB began to look like an impregnable defence. At his second World Championship match with Karpov at Merano 1981, Korchnoi tried out an entirely new tack against the Queen's Gambit Declined. That treatment is what Korchnoi repeats here against Short.

6 ... 0-0
7 ♖c1!? dxc4
8 e3

8 e4 is more aggressive. Korchnoi seems to be steering for simplification in which his greater experience might tell.

8 ... c5
9 ♗xc4 cxd4
10 ♘xd4

In Korchnoi-Karpov (9) Merano 1981, 10 exd4 led nowhere for White after 10 ... ♘c6 11 0-0 ♘h5 12 ♗xe7 ♘xe7 13 ♗b3 ♘f6 14 ♘e5 ♗d7 15 ♕e2 ♖c8 16 ♘e4 ♘xe4 17 ♕xe4 ♗c6. Much better would have been 16 ♖fe1! to meet 16 ... ♗c6 with 17 ♘xf7! ♖xf7 18 ♕xe6.

Korchnoi's choice here invites liquidation.

10 ... ♗d7
11 0-0

A slight variation from

135

Korchnoi-Karpov (17) 1981, where 11 ♗e2 ♘c6 12 ♘b3 ♘d5 13 ♗xe7 ♘cxe7 14 ♘xd5 ♘xd5 15 ♕d4 ♗c6 16 ♗f3 ♘e7 17 ♗xc6 ♘xc6 18 ♕xd8 ♖fxd8 19 ♔e2 rewarded Korchnoi with nothing more than an insipid draw.

11	...	♘c6
12	♘b3	♖c8
13	♗e2	♘d5

Short copies the Karpov method of trading pieces. The difference is that Black has ... ♖c8, while in this case White has castled.

14	♗xe7	♘cxe7
15	♘xd5	♘xd5
16	♖xc8	♕xc8
17	♕d4	

An insidious position. If White could organise an attack against Black's Q-side with ♖c1, e4-e5 and perhaps ♗f3, he would stand better, in spite of the symmetrical pawn structure.

However, Short acts resolutely to force immediate equality.

17	...	b6!
18	♖c1	♕b8
19	e4	♘f4
20	♗f1	♖d8

½:½

A good solid result for Short just after his sensational win v Kasparov.

GAME FOURTEEN
HÜBNER - NUNN

1 e4 e5 2 ♘f3 ♘c6 3 ♗b5 ♘d4 4 ♘xd4 ed
5 0-0 ♗c5 6 c3 c6 7 ♗a4 ♘e7 8 d3 d5 9 ♘d2
♗b6 10 cd ♘xd4 11 ♔h1 0-0 12 f4 f5 13 e5
b5 14 ♗b3 c5 15 ♘f3 ♘c6 16 a4 ♗a6 17
♘xd4 ♘xd4 18 ab ♗xb5 19 ♗e3 ♗e6 20
♕f3 ♗c6 21 ♖a6 ♕d7 22 ♖xc6 ♕xc6 23
♗xd5 ♕c8 24 ♖c1 ♖b8 25 ♖xc5 ♕d7 26
♖c6 ♖fe8 27 ♖d6 ♕f7 28 ♗c4 1:0

GAME FOURTEEN
HÜBNER · NUNN

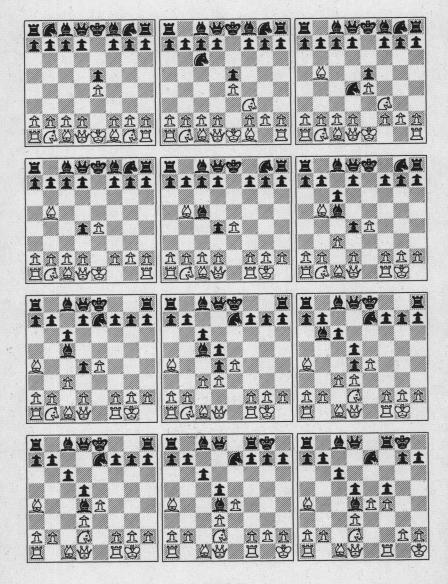

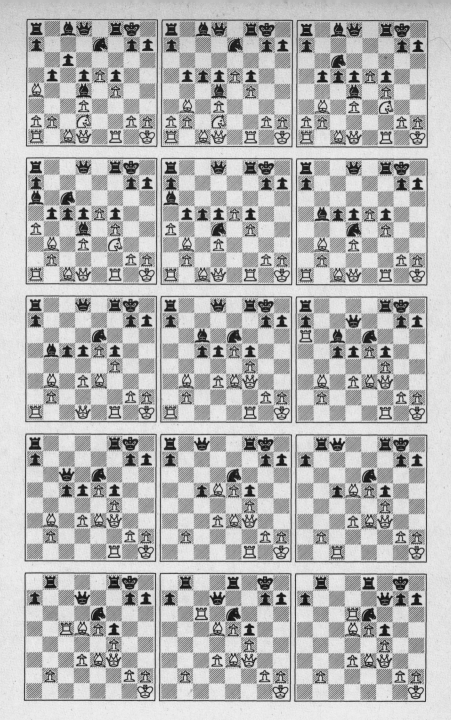

139

1:0

The Hübner-Nunn game shortly after the start.

Hübner - Nunn

1 e4	e5
2 ♘f3	♘c6
3 ♗b5	♘d4

Bird's Defence, a rare visitor to the shores of grandmaster chess. Blackburn relied on it at St. Petersburg 1914, losing to Capablanca, but drawing with Alekhine, after the latter blundered away a piece.

It is more usual to see John Nunn defending against the Lopez with the Marshall Gambit, or its offshoots.

4 ♘xd4	exd4
5 0-0	♗c5
6 c3	

Gipslis has suggested the extravagant 6 b4!? while the modern main line is considered to be: 6 d3 c6 7 ♗c4 d6 8 f4 ♘f6 9 e5 dxe5 10 ♗xf7+ ♔xf7 11 fxe5 ♕d5 12 exf6 gxf6 13 ♘d2 Kasparov - Roizman, USSR 1978.

6 ...	c6
7 ♗a4	

Hübner decides that he does not want his KB on c4 where it might be molested by ... d5. The German Grandmaster's conduct of the opening is not positionally ambitious in comparison with Kasparov's treatment cited above.

7 ...	♘e7
8 d3	d5
9 ♘d2	

Threatening ♘b3. If Black plays 9 ... dxc3 then 10 bxc4 dxe4 11 ♘xe4 cedes White the initiative.

9 ...	♗b6

Side-stepping the threat at the cost of a tempo.

10 cxd4	♗xd4
11 ♔h1	0-0
12 f4	f5

Nunn feels he must stop Hübner playing f5, cramping his K-side, even though White now obtains a protected passed pawn.

13 e5	

Nevertheless, Black's position seems sound enough. White's play here has not refuted the Bird. Black should now continue along strict blockading lines with 13 ... ♗e6 and ... ♕d7. Nimzovich's games and writings are full of such examples. Instead, Nunn tempts fate with active play.

13	...	b5?!
14	♗b3	c5
15	♘f3	♘c6
16	a4!	

Whatever Black does now is unsatisfactory, eg. 16 ... b4 — closing the Q-side — 17 a5 (threatening ♗a4) 17 ... ♘xa5 18 ♖xa5 ♕xa5 19 ♗xd5+ winning. Or 16 ... b4 17 a5 h6 18 a6 ♗e6 19 ♗a4 ♕b6 20 ♗xc6 ♕xc6 21 ♘xd4 cxd4 22 ♗d2 with pressure to come against the exposed Black pawns on b4 and d4. But what happens is no better.

16	...	♗a6?
17	♘xd4	♘xd4
18	axb5	♗xb5
19	♗e3	♘e6

19 ♘xb3 20 ♕xb3 wins at least a pawn for White.

20	♕f3	♗c6

20 ... ♗xd3 is hopeless after 21 ♗xd5.

| 21 | ♖a6! | |

This Rook invasion — a curious parallel to Nunn-Short — swiftly decides matters. Black's position cannot stand up to the strain being imposed from all directions.

21	...	♕d7
22	♖xc6!	♕xc6
23	♗xd5	♕c8
24	♖c1	

Even stronger than 24 ♗xc8.

24	...	♖b8
25	♖xc5	♕d7
26	♖c6	♖fe8
27	♖d6	♕f7
28	♗c4	

Black resigns. If 28 ... ♖xb2 29 ♖xe6 ♖b1+ 30 ♗g1 ♖xe6 31 ♕xa8+ is murderous.

GAME FIFTEEN
KASPAROV-PORTISCH

1 d4 ♘f6 2 c4 e6 3 ♘f3 d5 4 ♘c3 ♗e7 5 ♗g5
0-0 6 e3 ♘bd7 7 ♕c2 h6 8 cd ed 9 ♗f4 c5
10 ♗e2 b6 11 0-0 ♗b7 12 ♖fd1 ♖c8 13 dc
bc 14 a4 ♕a5 15 ♘h4 ♖fd8 16 ♘f5 ♗f8
17 ♘b5 ♗e8 18 ♗d6 ♘xd6 19 ♘fxd6 ♖b8
20 ♘xb7 ♖xb7 21 ♖xd5 ♖db8 22 ♕d2
♕xd2 23 ♖xd2 ♘f6 24 ♖a2 ♗e4 25 ♖c2
♖d7 26 g3 a5 27 ♔g2 g6 28 ♗f3 ♘f6 29 ♘a3
♗d6 30 ♘c6 ♖dd8 31 ♖a1 ♗e5 32 ♘b5
♘d5 33 ♖b1 ♗d6 34 ♖d2 ♘b6 35 ♖c1
♗e7 36 ♖e2 ♖bc8 37 ♘b1 ♔g7 38 ♘d2
♖a8 39 ♘b3 ♖dc8 40 ♖ec2 c4 41 ♘d2 ♖a7
42 ♘xc4 ♘xc4 43 ♖xc4 ♖xc4 44 ♖xc4 f5
45 h3 h5 46 g4 hg 47 hg fg 48 ♔g3 ♗d6+
49 ♔xg4 ♖c7 50 ♗c6 ♖f7 51 f4 ♔h6
52 ♗d5 ♖f6 53 ♖c1 ♔g7 54 b3 ♖f8 55 ♖d1
♗c5 56 ♖d3 ♗a3 57 ♗e4 ♗c1 58 ♖d7+
♔h6 59 ♖e7 ♗d2 60 ♔f3 ♗b4 61 ♖b7 ♗c3
62 ♗d3 ♖f6 63 ♔g4 ♗d2 64 f5 1:0

GAME FIFTEEN

KASPAROV-PORTISCH

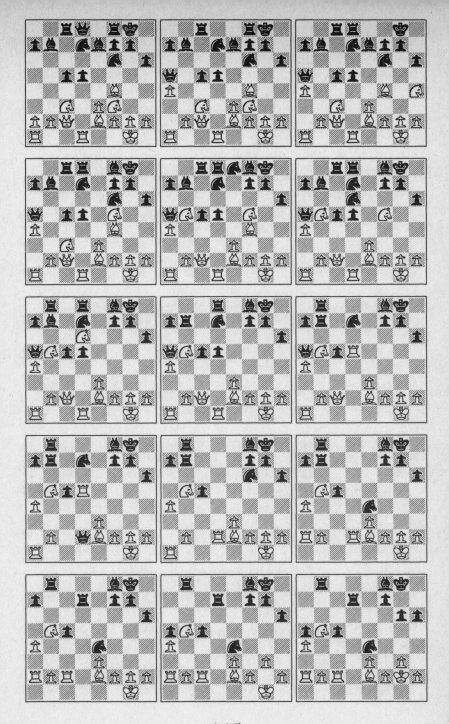

145

146

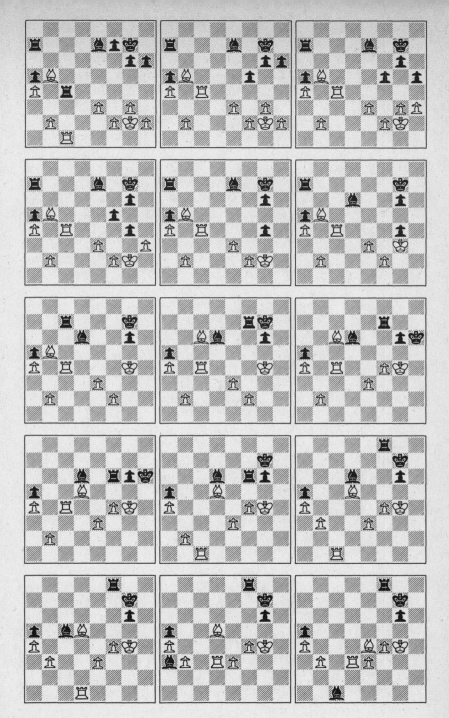

147

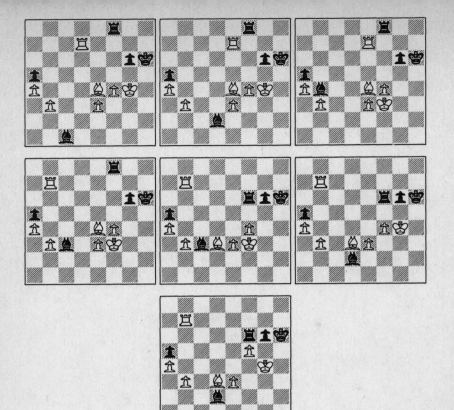

1:0

Kasparov - Portisch

1	d4	♘f6
2	c4	e6
3	♘f3	d5
4	♘c3	♗e7
5	♗g5	0-0
6	e3	♘bd7

Kasparov is clearly very familiar with the 6 ... h6 7 ♗xf6 line and Portisch steers the game into the calmer waters of the Classical variation. But you can always count on Kasparov to produce a surprise.

7	♕c2	h6!?

7 ... c5 may be better here. Black is mixing his systems.

8	cxd5!	

The exclamation mark is for effect. How many players would have thought of such a move? If now 8 ... hxg5 9 dxe6 fxe6 10 ♘xg5 ♘b6 White has two pawns and a strong attack for the piece.

Portisch shies away from any preanalysed complications — he must have been ready only for 8 h4!? which although is also in Kasparov's style, has been analysed more deeply.

8	...	exd5
9	♗f4	

After 9 ♗h4 c6 it's quite equal.

9	...	c5!?

Portisch plays his part in this interesting game. He clearly wants to deter long castling.

10	♗e2	b6
11	0-0	♗b7
12	♖fd1!	♖c8
13	dxc5	bxc5

So we reach a normal position with hanging pawns. There's no reason to suppose that White is anything other than a little better here, but Kasparov finds an original plan.

14 a4!

Pre-empting any thoughts Black might have had of ♘d7-b6

14 ...   ♕a5?!

With the idea of 15 ♕b3 ♗a6! but White is not compelled to do this. 14 ... ♖e8 intending ♘f8, ♗d6 was a solid and sensible plan, trying to cut down the activity of White's Bishop on f4.

15 ♘h4

Kasparov in his element; attacking the King.

15 ...   ♖fd8
16 ♘f5   ♗f8
17 ♘b5   ♘e8

Things are getting difficult for Portisch. Rather than try to destabilize the influence of the hanging pawns Kasparov has gone straight for the throat. He threatens an invasion on d6.

18 ♗d6

18 ...   ♘xd6
If 18 ... ♘ef6 then 19 ♘e7 ♗xe7 20 ♗xe7 ♖e8 21 ♗xf6 intending 22 ♘d6 +-. Or 18 ... ♘db8 19 ♘e7+ ♗xe7 20 ♗xe7 ♖d7 21 ♗xc5 a6 22 b4 ♕xb4 23 ♗xb4 ♖xc2 24 ♘d4 +-.
After 18 ... ♘xd6 Portisch surrenders his d-pawn, but he hopes to get counterplay on the b-file.

19 ♘fxd6   ♖b8
20 ♘xb7   ♖xb7
21 ♖xd5   ♖db8
22 ♕d2!

The transition to a more tranquil type of game frustrates the hopes of the Hungarian.

22 ...   ♕xd2
23 ♖xd2   ♘f6
24 ♖a2

And the technical phase begins. This may seem pretty dour but already both players were coming into time trouble. The new FIDE system of 40 moves in two hours and then 20 moves in one hour certainly provided its fair share of incident in this tournament.

24 ...   ♘e4
25 ♖c2   ♖d7
26 g3   a5
26 ... ♖bd8 27 a5
27 ♔g2   g6
28 ♗f3   ♘f6
29 ♘a3   ♗d6
30 ♗c6   ♖dd8
31 ♖a1   ♗e5
32 ♗b5   ♘d5
33 ♖b1   ♗d6
34 ♖d2   ♘b6

35	♖c1	♗e7	48 ...	♗d6+
36	♖e2	♖bc8	49 ♔xg4	♖c7
37	♘b1			

The only chance is to exchange Rooks. Kasparov is not interested.

Heavyweight manoeuvring but these positions are torture for the defender. When you know that you have absolutely no chance of winning it's very difficult.

| 50 | ♗c6 | ♖f7 |
| 51 | f4 | ♔h6 |

Portisch can only wait.

37	...	♔g7
38	♘d2	♖a8
39	♘b3	♖dc8
40	♖ec2	c4

40 ... ♖a7 41 ♘c5 ♖ac7 42 ♘e6+

41	♘d2	♖a7
42	♘xc4	♘xc4
43	♖xc4	♖xc4
44	♖xc4	f5

To avoid a White plan with f2-f4, e3-e4 and e4-e5. But despite the long job ahead for White to create a passed pawn it's difficult to believe that Black can save the game.

45	h3	h5
46	g4	hxg4
47	hxg4	fxg4
48	♔g3	

52	♗d5	♖f6
53	♖c1	♔g7
54	b3	♖f8
55	♖d1	♗c5
56	♖d3	♗a3
57	♗e4	♗c1
58	♖d7+	♔h6
59	♖e7	♗d2
60	♔f3	♗b4
61	♖b7	♗c3
62	♗d3	♖f6
63	♔g4	♗d2

63 ... ♖d6 64 ♗c4 intending 65 ♗g8

64 f5!
1:0

A tired Portisch has to throw in the towel. If:

a) 64 ... g5 then 65 e4 is +−

b) 64 ... ♗xe3 65 fxg6 ♖f4+ 66 ♔g3 ♖f8 67 ♖h7+ ♔g5 68 g7 intending 69 ♗c4 and 70 g8=♕

c) 64 ... ♖d6 65 ♗c4! intending 66 ♗g8.

KASPAROV-PORTISCH Rd 5

— The Players TV commentaries

1	d4	♘f6
2	c4	e6
3	♘f3	d5
4	♘c3	♗e7
5	♗g5	0-0
6	e3	

PORTISCH: I know that in this position Karpov and Kasparov played many games in which Black played 6 ... h6 and this position is probably well known to him. So why not try a very old line, ♘bd7. Once it was my favourite defence against the queen's gambit. Perhaps he's not prepared against it.

6 ... ♘bd7

KASPAROV: It's very strange, Portisch plays this very old variation. It's seldom seen in grandmaster practice nowadays. Maybe he has prepared something specially for this game. I can remember just one game of mine, I played 7 ♕c2 against Marovic seven years ago. Maybe Portisch prepared something, but I know a new idea too in this position.

7 ♕c2 h6

KASPAROV: Now there is the quiet line 8 ♗h4, which I have never played. It's too passive in my opinion. The sharp line 8 h4 I played

against Marović, and I won a beautiful game. But there is another way. The sharpest line is to sacrifice a piece after 8 cxd5 and if 8 ... hxg5 it's a very interesting position. Unfortunately I didn't analyse it too much. Anyway, I remembered the conclusion: it's a very strong attack, very dangerous. But to sacrifice a piece now is a big risk. Of course, I could lose. But how should I decide this problem? I should play like Kasparov if I want to win this game. I should take on d5. No choice.

8 cxd5

PORTISCH: What is this? He has been thinking for more than half an hour, but this is a piece sacrifice. Let me see, if I take it, it looks very simple: 8 ... hxg5 then 9 dxe6, I have to take back on e6, then ♘xg5. He has two pawns and an attack. I don't like it when he is attacking. But what is this? Is it a prepared variation or something he just discovered at the board. I have the feeling that it has been prepared. If I take back the pawn at d5, it's very safe. If he goes back to h4, I can equalise very simply with c6 followed by ♘e4. I have played many games like that already. But what happens if he goes back to f4? I don't like that position, but perhaps he won't do it. Anyway, if I accept the piece sacrifice maybe I will lose very quickly in a brilliant game. Oh, what should I do now. Well, maybe I had better take back the pawn. Accepting such a piece sacrifice needs more profound analysis.

8 ... exd5

KASPAROV: I was rather sure if he spent at least two minutes he would refuse to take the piece. People usually take pieces without hesitation. Of course, he was afraid of my home preparation. Portisch is used to being afraid of preparation because he spends himself a lot of time for the newest ideas in the openings. It's very strange why Portisch didn't know this line. Okay. I have no time to discuss that problem with myself. I must play ♘h4 or ♗f4. ♗f4 is more interesting, because it's a fresher line.

9 ♗f4

PORTISCH: I have to prevent his castling queen-side, now my kingside is very weak, and the only way to prevent it is by c5. Although then I will have an isolate pawn, but if he castles queen-side at least I will have attacking chances there.

9 ...c5

KASPAROV: Portisch found a new way, the usual move is c6. Now play very solid, very positional way. I have already given him the chance to take a piece. That's enough for me in this game. Now I should play ♗e2, 0-0, ♖d1 and push on this d-pawn in the centre.

10 ♗e2

PORTISCH: He didn't dare to castle queenside. It would have been a good chance for me. Now if I take the pawn at d4, I have this isolated pawn without any chance, so let's try b6.

10 ...   b6

11 0-0   ♗b7

KASPAROV: Now the problem - I should play ♖d1, but which rook? I think the rook from f1 is better because I can use the other rook for a very interesting idea, maybe nobody played it before.

12 ♖fd1   ♖c8

13 dxc5   bxc5

KASPAROV: Now the usual plan is to push against these pawns, especially the one on d5, but my idea is to try to use this square on f5. After ♘h4 he can't play g6 because of the pawn on h6. But now, ♘h4 is nothing. He plays even g5 or ♖e8. I should try to take his queen from d8. Now I can create a positional threat on the queenside because of this very important square b6. If my pawn can come to a5, it's very unpleasant for Black. After 14 a4, I have the positional threat ♘e5, and then ♗f3 and after ... ♘b6, I have a5. If he plays ... a5 himself, there's a very important square on b5 for my knight or my bishop. After a4, if he plays ♕a5, then my main threat will come.

14 a4

PORTISCH: What move is this? He's just weakening his queenside. Is that really so? Oh no, he's starting to push the pawn to a6 and taking away a very important square from my knight at b6. So I have to do something here. I don't like a6, because he will just play a5. I don't like ... a5 either, because it gives him a very strong square at b5. So I have to come out with my queen to a5. It's a good move. If he plays ♕b3 then I have ♗c6.

14 ...   ♕a5

KASPAROV: Of course Portisch didn't see the main threat in the position. Now I should play ♘h4.

15 ♘h4

PORTISCH: Pooh! I simply forgot about this. So ♕a5

wasn't as good as it looked. I shouldn't have forgotten about the penetration of this knight. I had already seen many games with the knight coming to f5. Now it's very difficult to prevent ♘f5 and I have a weak spot at d6. Anyway I have no other c h o i c e , I have to play ♖fd8.

15 ...   ♖fd8
16 ♘f5   ♗f8
17 ♘b5   ♘e8

KASPAROV: Portisch defends this square d6. I think he doesn't imagine my next move, because he's thinking about just ♘d6. I can put on this square another piece, my bishop. This is much more important, because there are many threats: ♘e7+ or ♗b7, or ♗xf8 and ♘d6. He can't defend his pawns. It's a very unusual move. It's beautiful. It's very good strategy in the opening.

18 ♗d6

PORTISCH: Unfortunately this is very strong. I cannot take it because simply I'm going to lose a pawn, but if I don't take it, what happens? ... No, I have to take at d6 anyway. Maybe it's the best chance to give up a pawn and hope for opposite coloured bishops.

18 ...   ♘xd6
19 ♘fxd6   ♖b8

20	♘xb7	♖xb7
21	♖xd5	♖db8
22	♕d2	♕xd2
23	♖xd2	

KASPAROV: Now we have an endgame. In the next moves, I will protect my pawn on b2 with two rooks, on a2 and then maybe ♖c2 and improve the position of my king; try to put my knight on c4, or maybe play a5. If he plays a5 himself, I play ♘a3, maybe my bishop will come to b5. Then with my knight on c4 I can try to attack his weaknesses on a5 and c5. Of course it should be winning, but after many moves.

23 ... ♘f6 24 ♖a2 ♘e4 25 ♖c2 ♖d7 26 g3 a5 27 ♔g2 g6 28 ♗f3 ♘f6 29 ♘a3 ♗d6 30 ♗c6 ♖dd8 31 ♖a1 ♗e5 32 ♗b5 ♘d5 33 ♖b1 ♗d6 34 ♖d2 ♘b6 35 ♖c1 ♗e7 36 ♖e2 ♖bc8 37 ♘b1 ♔g7 38 ♘d2 ♖a8 39 ♘b3 ♖dc8 40 ♖ec2 c4 41 ♘d2 ♖a7 42 ♘xc4 ♗xc4 43 ♖xc4 ♖xc4 44 ♖xc4

PORTISCH: Now we have this unpleasant ending. I wish I could exchange rooks, then I have drawing chances. But everybody knows that in such an ending nobody who has the advantage will exchange rooks. He will just push the pawns in the centre. I have to stop him playing f4, e4, e5 or I will be crushed, so I have to play f5.

44 . . .f5

KASPAROV: Now it's a very important problem how many pawns on the kingside I should exchange. It feels better to have as many pawns as possible when you have a material advantage in the endgame. But if I exchange two pawns I can keep a very important position for my king on g4. Then I can improve mypawns, play f4, e4, e5 and attack his pawn on g6. This is very important. h3.

45 h3 h5 46 g4 hxg4 47 hxg4 fxg4 48 ♔g3 ♗d6+ 49 ♔xg4 ♖c7 50 ♗c6 ♖f7 51 f4 ♔h6 52 ♗d5 ♖f6 53 ♖c1 ♔g7 54 b3 ♖f8 55 ♖d1 ♗c5 56 ♖d3 ♗a3 57 ♗e4 ♗c1 58 ♖d7+ ♔h6 59 ♖e7 ♗d2 60 ♔f3 ♗b4 61 ♖b7 ♗c3 62 ♘d3 ♖f6 63 ♔g4 ♗d2 64 f5

PORTISCH: Oh, that's why I shouldn't have attacked that pawn. So what is this, Oh yes, if I take gxf5 then ♗xf5 and there is mate. So, I can seal this move, that's the referee already bringing the envelope, so I can seal ♗xe3. But what to God is this stupid thing? I think I should resign this position. Why adjourn it as many people do? Why not give my opponent the joy of victory when he deserves it.   1:0

ROUND SIX:

Game No.16	Short	1:0	Portisch
Game No.17	Kasparov	1:0	Nunn
Game No.18	Hübner	1:0	Korchnoi

A round of extremes, with two long games and one remarkably quick one. The quickie was Kasparov's win against Nunn. Most of this game must have been analysed by the world champion as part of his world championship preparation. Short's win against Portisch was a fine positional achievement, showing how much the English grandmaster's style has matured over the past year or two. Hübner continued his recovery at the expense of Korchnoi. At the adjournment (move 61) Hübner was unsure whether the position could be won, but on resumption Korchnoi missed the most testing defence.

SCORES: Kasparov 4½; Short 4; Korchnoi, Hübner & Portisch 2½; Nunn 2.

At this stage, it looked possible that we might see a real race between Kasparov and Short for first place. Nobody could have guessed that Short would, in fact, score no more points at all.

GAME SIXTEEN
SHORT-PORTISCH

1 e4 e5 2 ♘f3 ♘c6 3 ♗c4 ♗c5 4 c3 ♘f6 5 b4
♗b6 6 d3 a6 7 0-0 d6 8 ♘bd2 0-0 9 ♗b3 ♘e7
10 ♖e1 ♘g6 11 h3 ♗e6 12 ♘c4 ♗a7 13 ♗e3
♗xe3 14 ♖xe3 h6 15 d4 ♕e7 16 ♕e1 ♘h7
17 ♖d1 ♖ad8 18 ♘a5 ♗c8 19 ♔h2 ♘f4 20
de de 21 ♘c4 ♖xd1 22 ♕xd1 ♖d8 23 ♕c2
♘g6 24 ♖d3 ♖xd3 25 ♕xd3 ♘f6 26 g3 ♗d7
27 ♘e3 ♗b5 28 ♗c4 ♗c6 29 ♘d2 ♘e8 30
♗d5 ♗xd5 31 ed ♘f6 32 ♘e4 ♘xe4 33
♕xe4 ♘f8 34 ♘f5 ♕f6 35 c4 h5 36 ♔g2 g6
37 ♘e3 ♘h7 38 h4 ♕e7 39 c5 ♘f6 40 ♕c4
e4 41 ♕d4 ♕d8 42 ♕e5 b6 43 c6 ♘e8 44
♕xe4 ♘d6 45 ♕e5 b5 46 g4 hg 47 h5 ♔h7
48 ♘xg4 ♕h4 49 ♕f4 g5 50 ♘f6+ ♔g7 51
♕xh4 gh 52 ♘d7 ♘f5 53 ♘b8 ♘e7 54 ♘xa6
♘xd5 55 ♔h3 ♔f6 56 ♔xh4 ♔f5 57 a3 f6 58
f3 ♘e6 59 ♔g4 ♘e3+ 60 ♔f4 ♘d5+ 61
♔e4 f5 62 ♔d4 ♔d6 63 h6 ♘f6 64 ♘xc7 1:0

GAME SIXTEEN

SHORT-PORTISCH

160

161

162

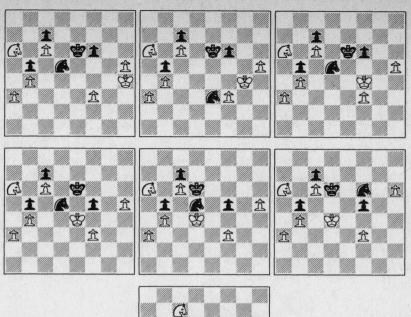

1:0

GAME SIXTEEN

Short - Portisch

1 e4	e5
2 ♘f3	♘c6
3 ♗c4	

It seems unlikely that such an antiquated choice should bother a modern Grandmaster of Portisch's stature, but it should not be forgotten that in 1981 Karpov severely tested Korchnoi with two Italians in their world title match.

If handled slowly and patiently White can sometimes hold a small but signifant advantage in terrain. Further, Short's style, at its best, approximates quite closely to the pythonesque manoeuvres of Karpov.

3 ...	♗c5
4 c3	♘f6
5 b4	

This is more likely to succeed than the premature explosion of energy resulting from 5 d4.

5 ...	♗b6
6 d3	a6

To provide a haven for his KB on a7.

7 0-0	d6
8 ♘bd2	0-0
9 ♗b3	♘e7
10 ♖e1	♘g6

Black's Knights are aggressively posted on the K-side but they lack permanent advance outposts; viz, a Knight landing on f4 can eventually be evicted by means of g3.

11 h3	♗e6
12 ♘c4!	

Black's QB is a problem piece in this opening, so White does not exchange with 12 ♗xe6 fxe6 which would also cede Black an open f-file.

12 ...	♗a7
13 ♗e3!	

The other side of the coin. Black can scarcely avoid this exchange.

13 ...	♗xe3
14 ♖xe3	

14 fxe3 no longer fits in with White's strategic dispositions, after he has played b4 and ♖e1.

14 ...	h6
15 d4	

Staking a claim to the initiative which he never relinquishes.

15 ... Qe7
16 Qe1 Nh7
17 Rd1 Rad8
18 Na5 Bc8
19 Kh2 Nf4

At last, but Black's triumph is short-lived.

20 dxe5 dxe5
21 Nc4 Rxd1
22 Qxd1 Rd8
23 Qc2 Ng6

Forced retreat to defend e5.

24 Rd3

To reduce counterplay White trades Rooks. In the ensuing endgame of Queens plus minor pieces, Short enjoys some notable advantages:

i) Greater control of Q-side space based on his b4 pawn. Also, potential Q-side pawn mass-mobility;

ii) Superior co-ordination within his own position based on invulnerability to Black minor piece incursions on d4 or f4 (respectively the key squares in both camps);

iii) a real chance of invading the Black position on d5 or f5.

24 ... Rxd3
25 Qxd3 Nf6
26 g3!

A first important step towards restriction of Black's Knight.

26 ... Bd7
27 Ne3 Bb5
28 Bc4 Bc6
29 Nd2 Ne8
30 Bd5 Bxd5
31 exd5

The second step. White has created a mobile pawn majority in the centre and on the Q-wing. Perhaps Black should have avoided 30 ... Bxd5, but he is hard pressed for other constructive moves.

31 ... Nf6
32 Ne4 Nxe4
33 Qxe4 Nf8
34 Nf5 Qf6
35 c4 h5

Threatening ... g6, which was not previously possible on account of 36 Nxh6+ and Ng4.

36 Kg2 g6
37 Ne3 Nh7
38 h4

To stop ... Ng5.

38 ... Qe7
39 c5 Nf6
40 Qc4 e4

To get some breathing space, but the pawn becomes weak and the white Queen finds a pleasant square on d4.

41 Qd4 Qd8
42 Qe5 b6

Introducing a plan to blockade the white position at the cost of a pawn.

43 c6

43 ...   ♘e8

A critical moment. If 43 ... ♔f8 44 d6 ♕xd6 45 ♕xd6 cxd6 46 c7 wins. Or 44 ... cxd6 45 c7! ♕xc7 46 ♕xf6.

So now is the time to give up the pawn while White's Q-side armada has temporarily forfeited its mobility.

44 ♕xe4   ♘d6
45 ♕e5   b5
46 g4

Blasting open the position and leading by force to a won Knight and pawn ending.

46 ...   hxg4
47 h5   ♔h7
48 ♘xg4   ♕h4
49 ♕f4

The threat of ♘f6+ leaves Black little choice.

49 ...   g5
50 ♘f6+   ♔g7
51 ♕xh4   gxh4
52 ♘d7   ♘f5
53 ♘b8   ♘e7
54 ♘xa6   ♘xd5

Both Knights are immobilised by their relationship to the pawn on c7, so what follows is

effectively a King and pawn ending.

55 ♔h3   ♔f6
56 ♔xh4   ♔f5
57 a3   f6
58 f3   ♔e6
59 ♔g4   ♘e3+
60 ♔f4   ♘d5+
61 ♔e4   f5+
62 ♔d4   ♔d6
63 h6   ♘f6
64 ♘xc7!

Black resigns.

64 ... ♔xc7 65 ♔e5 ♘h7 66 ♔xf5 ♔c6 67 ♔g6 ♘f8+ 68 ♔f7 ♘h7 69 ♔g7 ♘g5 70 f4 ♘e6+ 71 ♔f6 ♘f8 72 ♔f7 ♘h7 73 ♔g7 wins Black's Knight.

GAME SEVENTEEN
KASPAROV-NUNN

1 d4 ♘f6 2 ♘f3 g6 3 c4 ♗g7 4 g3 0-0 5 ♗g2
c6 6 ♘c3 d5 7 cd cd 8 ♘e5 e6 9 0-0 ♘fd7
10 f4 ♘xe5 11 fe ♘c6 12 e4 de 13 ♗e3 f5
14 ef ♖xf6 15 ♘xe4 ♖xf1+ 16 ♕xf1 ♘xd4
17 ♖d1 e5 18 ♘g5 1:0

OFF THE BOARD

A world champion is allowed by tournament organisers certain minor eccentricities denied to lessor mortals.

Before each round, the tournament refrigerator was checked for the mandatory 12 bottles of tonic water (Kasparov, Gary, for the use of) and a quantity of Swiss chocolate. In each case, a particular proprietary brand was specified.

Kasparov was sufficiently particular that, when his last bar of chocolate vanished from under his nose, he complained loud and long. On enquiry, it proved that a hungry Nigel Short had seen the chocolate *en pris* and devoured it *en passant*.

"Whatever next?" said the rueful Kasparov. "First he beats me, then he scoffs my chocolate".

GAME SEVENTEEN

KASPAROV-NUNN

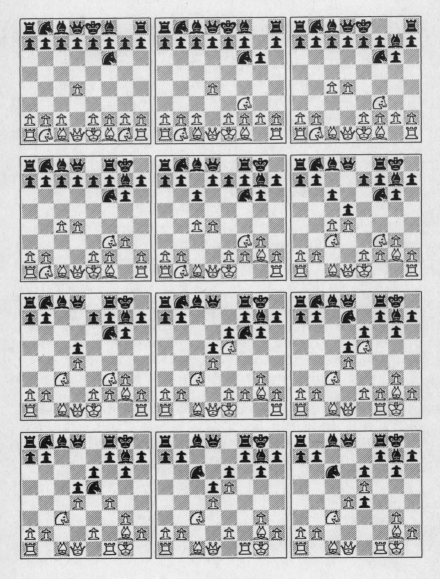

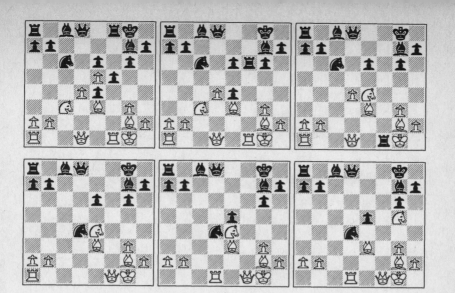

1:0

Kasparov - Nunn

1	d4	♘f6
2	♘f3	g6
3	c4	♗g7
4	g3	0-0
5	♗g2	c6

Varying from his habitual King's Indian, John Nunn opts for the stability and relative security of the super-solid Neo-Grünfeld. Kasparov used it himself twice in the recent world title match (games 3 and 13).

6 ♘c3

Note the importance of this move order, which establishes early pressure in the centre, especially against d5 and e4, rather than the stereotyped and more feeble 6 0-0.

6 ... d5

Of course, 6 ... d6 is also possible, reverting to the King's Indian.

7	cxd5	cxd5
8	♘e5!	e6
9	0-0	♘fd7
10	f4	

It is gradually emerging that this support for the outpost on e5 is the most ingenious way for White to aspire to any opening initiative in this symmetrical line.

I am fascinated by the fact that this variation, which has had a rather boring reputation in the past, suddenly seems to become hyper-tactical and theoretical once Kasparov becomes involved.

10 ... ♘xe5

Important. Nunn, as in his earlier game with Portisch, tries to solve his problems by very direct means, viz: the prompt removal of White's well placed Knight. Kasparov (13) v Karpov preferred the lengthy battle of manoeuvre resulting from 10 ... f6.

11 fxe5

The real point of White's play is committing himself to 10 f4. Portisch was less successful with 11 dxe5 which was met by ... ♛b6+(!) before White could carry out his strategy of ♗c3-f2 and e4.

11 ... ♘c6

12	e4	dxe4
13	♗e3	f5

Otherwise White has a dominating position after the unchallenged ♘xe4.

14	exf6 *ep*	♖xf6

15 ♘xe4!

Kasparov's innovation, and a typical pawn sacrifice for his active style. Unbeknown to both (!) players this whole variation had earlier been tested in a Swedish correspondence game between Gunnar Hjort and Mats Andersson. This reminds me of the case when Karpov introduced a brilliant new move in the English Opening against Timman at Montul 1979 (1 c4 e5 2 ♘c3 ♘f6 3 ♘f3 ♘c6 4 e3 ♗e7 5 d4 exd4 6 ♘xd4 0-0 7 ♘xc6 bxc6 8 ♗e2 d5 9 0-0 ♗d6 10 b3 ♕e7 11 ♗b2 and now Karpov uncorked 11 ... dxc4!!). Then everyone discovered it (11 ... dxc4!!) had originally been played by two Norwegian Corres-

pondence players. You just have to keep watching those Scandinavian Vikings when they play by post.

Sveshnikov-Mikhailcisin, Lvov 1983 had gone 15 ♖xf6 ♗xf6 16 ♘e2. Not very dynamic — just defending the pawn. No, that's not for Kasparov, or for Gunnar Hjort for that matter.

15	...	♖xf1+

Or 15 ... ♖f5 16 g4.

16	♕xf1	♘xd4

If 16 ... ♗xd4 17 ♗xd4 ♕xd4+ 18 ♔h1 with moves like ♖d1 and ♘f6+ in the air. Of course, Black must not take the pawn. (... h6 is worth a thought, to stop incursions on g5) but Black's position clearly holds promise.

17	♖d1	e5
18	♘g5!	

Resigns. A stunning miniature.

Kasparov demonstrated 18 ... ♕e7 19 ♗d5+ ♗e6 20 ♖xd4 exd4 21 ♗e6+ ♔h8

171

22 ♘f7+ ♚g8 23 ♘d8+ ♚h8 24 ♗g5! ♕b4 25 ♘f7+ ♚g8 26 ♘e5+ ♚h8 27 ♘xg6+ (to be followed by ♕h3) which was exactly the course of Hjort — M. Andersson!

Nunn's lifetime score against Kasparov is now 0/3, averaging a little over 20 moves!

Nunn applauds, Portisch looks the other way, but something else has captured Kasparov's attention.

GAME EIGHTEEN

HÜBNER - KORCHNOI

1 e4 e6 2 d4 d5 3 Nd2 c5 4 ed Qxd5 5 Ngf3
cd 6 Bc4 Qd6 7 0-0 Nf6 8 Nb3 Nc6 9
Nbxd4 Nxd4 10 Nxd4 a6 11 Bb3 Qc7 12
Qf3 Bd6 13 h3 0-0 14 Bg5 Nd7 15 c3 b5 16
Rad1 Bb7 17 Qg4 Kh8 18 Rfe1 Ne5 19
Qh5 Ng6 20 Bc2 Qg8 21 Nf3 Bxf3 22
Qxf3 Bh2+ 23 Kh1 Bf4 24 Bxf4 Nxf4 25
Rd4 Ng6 26 Red1 Rad8 27 a4 Rxd4 28
Rxd4 Rd8 29 Rxd8+ Qxd8 30 ab ab 31
Qe3 Qd5 32 Qd3 Qg5 33 b4 h6 34 g3 Qe5
35 Kg2 f5 36 Bb3 Ne7 37 Qd4 Qe2 38
Bd1 Qe1 39 Bf3 Kf7 40 Qc5 Qf6 41 c4 bc
42 Qxc4 Qd2 43 b5 Qd6 44 Qc3+ Kf7 45
Bh5+ g6 46 Bf3 h5 47 Qe3 Nc8 48 Bc6
Ne7 49 Bf3 Nc8 50 h4 Qb6 51 Qe5 Na7 52
Be2 Nc8 53 Bc4 Ne7 54 Qf3 Nc8 55 Ke2
Ne7 56 Qe3 Nd5 57 Qxb6 Nxb6 58 Kd3
Ke7 59 Kc3 Kd7 60 Bb4 Kd6 61 Ba2 Nc8
62 Ka5 Ke5 63 f4+ Kd6 64 Ka6 e5 65 Bf7
1:0

GAME EIGHTEEN

HÜBNER · KORCHNOI

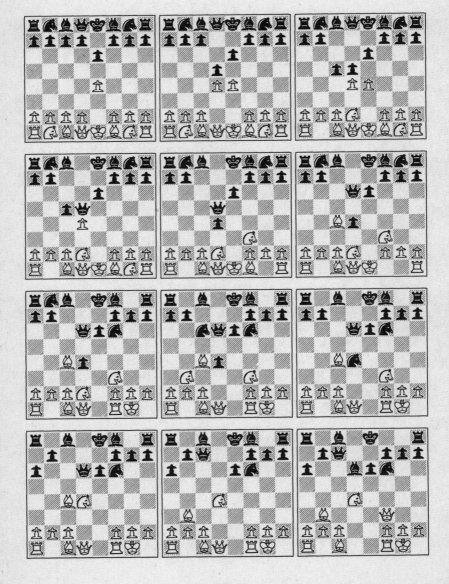

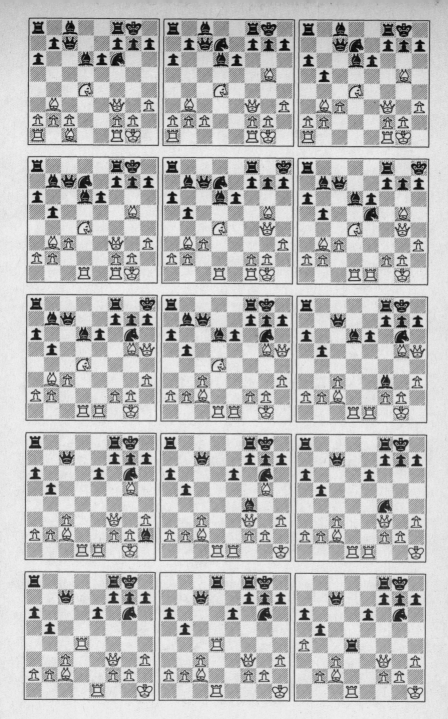

175

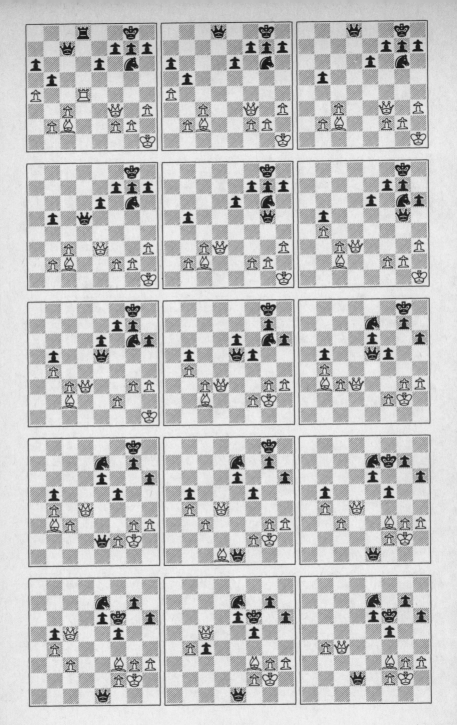

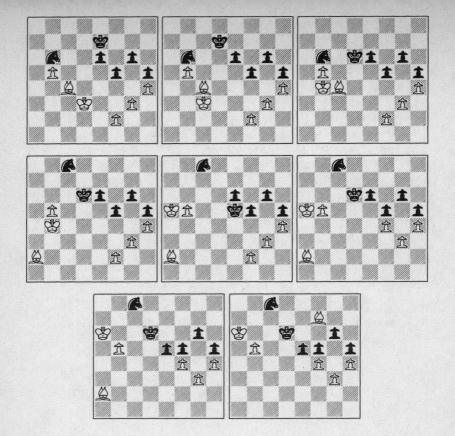

1:0

178

GAME EIGHTEEN

Hübner · Korchnoi

1	e4	e6
2	d4	d5
3	♘d2	

As befits a disciple of Dr Tarrasch, Hübner employs the Doctor's eponymous variation. Indeed, the temporary gambit which soon ensues was one of Tarrasch's favourite lines for White.

3	...	c5
4	exd5	♕xd5

A favourite alternative to Korchnoi's habitual 4 ... exd5. Black avoids the IQP, but suffers from a slight deficiency in development.

5	♘gf3	cxd4
6	♗c4	♕d6
7	0-0	♘f6
8	♘b3	♘c6
9	♘bxd4	♘xd4
10	♘xd4	a6
11	♗b3	♕c7
12	♕f3	♗d6

There are now exciting variations after 13 ♗g5!? offering his h2 pawn. Hübner prefers to rely on the technical future of the position to give him an advantage.

13	h3	0-0
14	♗g5	♘d7
15	c3	b5
16	♖ad1	

16 ♕xa8? ♗b7 17 ♕a7 ♗c5 favours Black, as does 17 ♕xf8+, since Black's Queen would be more active than White's Rook in the middlegame.

16	...	♗b7
17	♕g4	♔h8
18	♖fe1	♘e5
19	♕h5	♘g6

Not 19 ... ♘c4? 20 ♗c2! with a dangerous attack.

20	♗c2	♔g8
21	♘f3	♗xf3

Korchnoi sees a way to bring about mass exchanges, but Hübner still retains a tiny endgame edge.

22	♕xf3	♗h2+
23	♔h1	♗f4
24	♗xf4	♘xf4
25	♖d4	♘g6
26	♖ed1	

Black must now challenge White's Rooks.

the b5 pawn remains a target.

36	♗b3	♘e7
37	♕d4	♕e2

Not 37 ... ♕xd4 38 ♗xe6+.

38	♗d1	♕e1
39	♗f3	♔f7
40	♕c5	♔f6
41	c4	

White cannot win the pawn on b5 'for free', and he resolves instead to create a passed b-pawn.

41	...	bxc4
42	♕xc4	♕d2
43	b5	♕d6

26	...	♖ad8
27	a4	♖xd4
28	♖xd4	♖d8
29	♖xd8+	♕xd8
30	axb5	axb5
31	♕e3	

But White emerges from the slaughter with a tangible plus, even though it is very difficult to convert. White's advantage resides in the following features:

a) Black's b5 pawn is isolated and weak;

b) White has a potential passed pawn on the Q-file.;

c) White's Bishop is more mobile than Black's Knight.

But weaving these advantages into a win against Korchnoi is a real work of art.

31	...	♕d5
32	♕d3	♕g5
33	b4	

Fixing b5.

33	...	h6
34	g3	♕e5
35	♔g2	f5

Korchnoi tries to mobilise his own pawn majority, but

The next question is, how to shift Black's blockade over the b6 square.

44	♕c3+	♔f7
45	♗h5+	

An important check. Black must parry with ... g6, when a fresh weakness springs up in his camp. Just how significant this is will become apparent after the inevitable swap of Queens, when Black's entire K-side pawn constellation can ultimately not be protected against White's predatory Bishop.

45	...	g6
46	♗f3	h5
47	♕e3	♘c8
48	♗c6	♘e7
49	♗f3	♘c8
50	h4!	

After a period of hesitation Hübner hits on the correct plan.

The first stage is to nail down Black's pawns on light squares as future prey for the Bishop; then White transfers his Bishop to the a2-g8 diagonal, while finally Hübner centralises his King, in order to be able to offer a Queen exchange from e3. The final manoeuvre will break the Black blockade over b6.

| 50 | ... | ♕b6 |
| 51 | ♕e5 | |

White defers the trade of Queens until his Bishop is on the appropriate diagonal. The centralisation of the White Queen also impedes any movement of Black's King towards the Q-side.

51	...	♘a7
52	♗e2	♘c8
53	♗c4	♘e7
54	♔f3	♘c8
55	♔e2	♘e7
56	♕e3	♘d5
57	♕xb6	♘xb6
58	♔d3	

Black can not exchange on c4, so White wins the decisive tempo to penetrate with his King.

58	...	♔e7
59	♔c3	♔d7
60	♔b4	♔d6
61	♗a2	♘c8
62	♔a5	♔e5
63	f4 +	♔d6
64	♔a6	e5
65	♗f7	

Black resigns.

ROUND SEVEN

Game No.19	Hübner	1:0	Short
Game No.20	Korchnoi	½:½	Kasparov
Game No.21	Nunn	1:0	Portisch

Hübners third successive win put an effective end to Short's ambitions of first place. It was a miserable game for Short, who fell victim to Hübner's best constricting technique. After a bad opening, Short found himself firmly sat upon for the whole game. There was a brief flurry of excitement in Korchnoi-Kasparov before the position settled down to a draw. The old warrior seemed satisfied to have made two draws with the young champion. After sharing the lead after four rounds, Portisch had now lost three consecutive games. Kasparov claimed that the Hungarian was still in shock from 8 cxd5 in their game. He certainly put up little resistance against Nunn. Portisch was to lose the next two games also.

SCORES: Kasparov 5; Short 4; Hübner 3½;
Korchnoi and Nunn 3; Portisch 2½.

GAME NINETEEN

HÜBNER - SHORT

1 d4 Nf6 2 c4 e6 3 Nf3 d5 4 Nc3 Be7 5 Bf4
0-0 6 e3 c5 7 dc Bxc5 8 a3 Nc6 9 Qc2 Qa5
10 Nd2 Be7 11 Rd1 e5 12 Bg5 d4 13 Nb3
Qd8 14 Be2 h6 15 Bxf6 Bxf6 16 0-0 a5 17
Bf3 Bd7 18 Nc5 Be8 19 Nd5 Be7 20 Nd3
de 21 fe f5 22 Nxe7+ Qxe7 23 Bd5+ Kh8
24 Qc3 e4 25 Nf4 Rf6 26 c5 Rc8 27 b4 ab
28 ab Na7 29 Bc4 Bf7 30 Nd5 Bxd5 31
Rxd5 Rcf8 32 b5 Qe8 33 Re5 Qb8 34 Qd4
b6 35 c6 Rxc6 36 Rexf5 Rxf5 37 Rxf5 Rd6
38 Qxe4 Rd1+ 39 Bf1 Qd8 40 Rf7 Nxb5
41 Qg4 Rxf1+ 42 Rxf1 Nd6 43 Qd4 Qc7
44 Rf8+ Kh7 45 Qd3+ g6 46 Qd4 Nf7 47
h3 h5 48 Qf6 Qc1+ 49 Kh2 Qc7+ 50 Qf4
Ne5 51 Re8 1:0

GAME NINETEEN

HÜBNER - SHORT

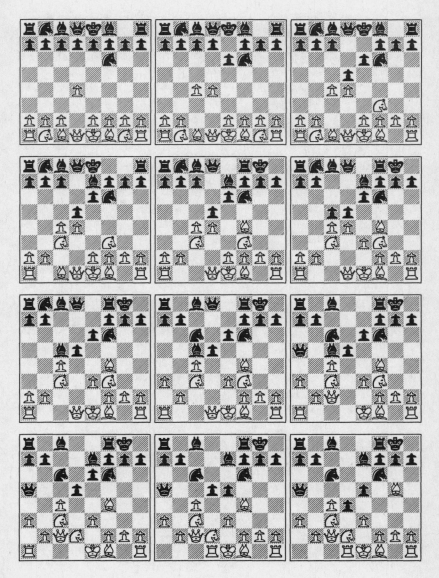

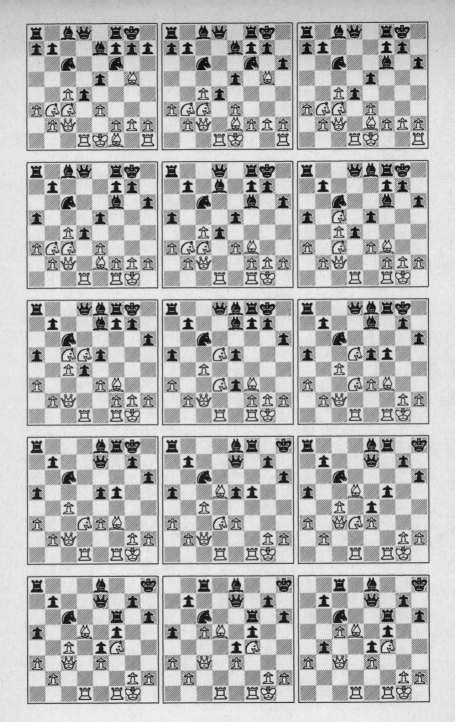

186

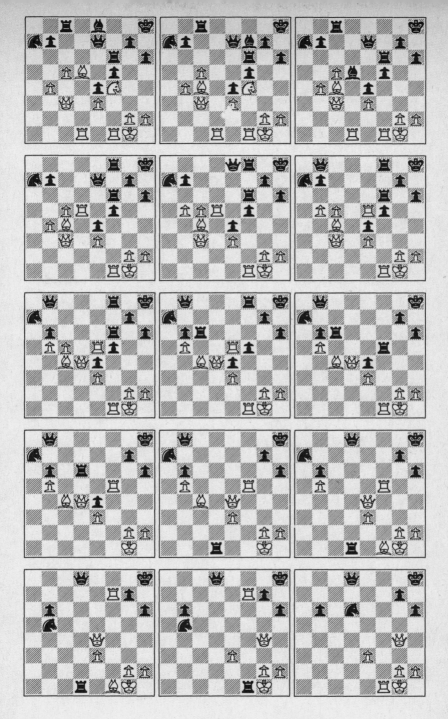

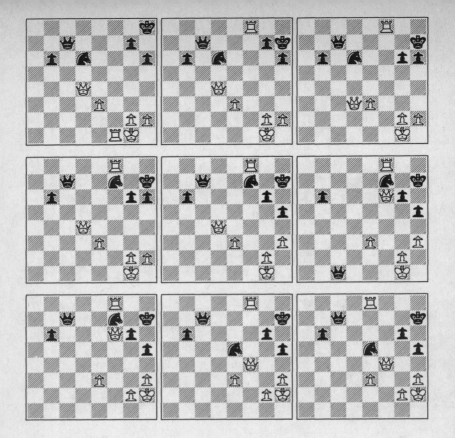

1:0

Hübner - Short

1	d4	♘f6
2	c4	e6
3	♘f3	d5
4	♘c3	♗e7
5	♗f4	0-0
6	e3	c5
7	dxc5	♗xc5
8	a3	♘c6
9	♕c2	♕a5
10	♘d2	♗e7
11	♖d1	e5
12	♗g5	d4
13	♘b3	♕d8
14	♗e2	h6?!

All theory so far and 14 ... a5 is considered to be a better move. Short has a new idea in mind.

| 15 | ♗xf6 | ♗xf6 |
| 16 | 0-0 | a5 |

Black is trying to weaken the pressure on his d4 pawn but unfortunately, his pawn on a4 will be even more vulnerable. 16 ... ♗e6 is a solid alternative to the text.

17 ♗f3!

Hübner lures the White pawns forward and then he will pick them off.

17 ... ♗d7

Unpinning. Nigel sees that his first idea is now impossible, eg. 17 ... a4? 18 ♘c5! ♗e7 19 ♘3xa4 ♕a5 20 b4 ♕a7 21 ♗xc6 + − and the second try to get a5-a4 in, fails as well, eg. 17 ... ♗e7 18 ♘a4! + − with a grip on the position.

18 ♘c5 ♗e8

The strength of Hübners Bishop is beginning to be felt. This is particularly apparent in the variation 18 ... b6? 19 ♘xd7 ♕xd7 20 ♕a4 ♖ac8 21 exd4 exd4 22 ♘d5 ♕d8 23 ♗g4. After the alternative 18 ... ♗e7 White takes the money and runs, eg. 19 ♘xb7! ♕b8 (19 ... ♕c7 20 ♘d5) 20 ♘d5 ♗xa3 21 bxa3 ♕xb7 22 ♘e7 + ♔h8 23 ♘xc6 ♗xc6 24 ♗xc6 ♕xc6 25 ex4 and Black is lost.

19 ♘d5

The pressure on Black's centre is becoming immense. White's advanced Knights prevent an adequate defence.

19 ...   &e7
20 &d3   dxe3?

Giving the Rook on f1 something to do. Maybe 20 ... &h8 or 20 ... f5 can be played but the latter looks dangerous after 21 &xe7+ &xe7 22 &d5+ &f7 23 &xc6 bxc6 24 exd4 exd4 25 &fe1.

21 fxe3   f5
22 &xe7+

Well timed. Black's centre looks strong but is, in fact, a liability.

22 ...   &xe7
23 &d5+   &h8
24 &c3   e4
25 &f4   &f6
26 c5!

Hübner neatly frustrates Short's idea of b7-b6 and Black's position is left static and prospectless.

26 ...   &c8
27 b4!   axb4
28 axb4   &a7
29 &c4   &f7
30 &d5   &xd5
31 &xd5   &cf8
32 b5   &e8

This is desperate defence. Once White creates a passed pawn on the queenside the game will be technically over.

33 &e5   &b8
34 &d4   b6
35 c6

35 ...   &xc6
36 &exf5   &xf5
37 &xf5

A typical transition of advantages. Hübner trades his queenside for a winning attack.

37 ...   &d6
38 &xe4   &d1+
39 &f1   &d8
40 &f7   &xb5
41 &g4   &xf1+

190

42	♖xf1	♘d6		48	♕f6	♕c1+
43	♕d4	♕c7		49	♔h2	♕c7+
44	♖f8+	♔h7		50	♕f4	♘e5
45	♕d3+	g6		51	♖e8	
46	♕d4	♘f7		1:0		
47	h3	h5				

Left to right: Hübner, Nunn,
Kasparov, Short, Korcnnoi, Portisch.

GAME TWENTY

KORCHNOI - KASPAROV

1 d4 d5 2 c4 e6 3 ♘c3 ♝e7 4 ♝f4 ♘f6 5 e3
0-0 6 ♖c1 c5 7 dxc5 ♝xc5 8 cxd5 exd5 9 ♘f3
♘c6 10 ♝e2 ♝e6 11 0-0 ♖c8 12 ♘b5 ♘e4
13 ♘d2 ♝xd2 14 ♛xd2 ♝b4 15 ♛d1 ♛b6
16 a3 ♝e7 17 b4 a5 18 ♘d6 ♖cd8 19 ♘xb7
♛xb7 20 b5 ♖c8 21 bxc6 ♖xc6 22 ♖b1
♖b6 23 ♖xb6 ♛xb6 24 ♝e5 ½:½

GAME TWENTY

KORCHNOI - KASPAROV

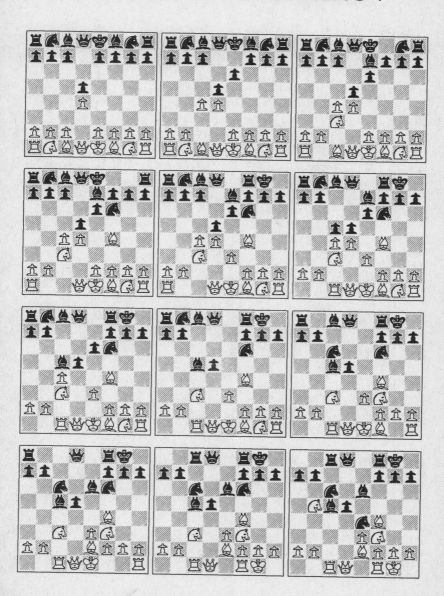

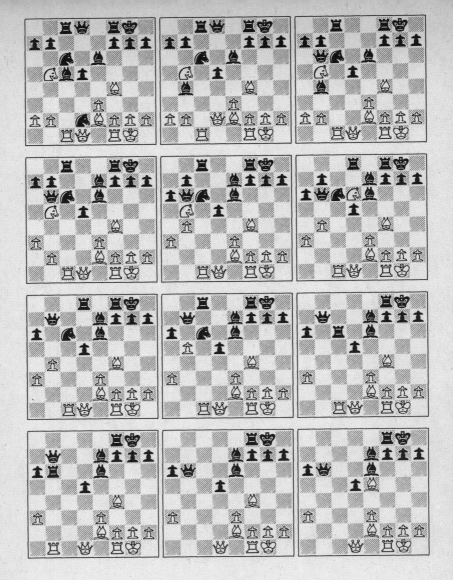

$$1/2 : 1/2$$

Korchnoi - Kasparov

1	d4	d5
2	c4	e6
3	♘c3	♗e7

At the Dubai Olympiad just before OHRA as in his first game here v Hübner, Kasparov continued to defend against 1 d4 with the Grünfeld. This, in spite of the three losses to Karpov in the 1986 World Championship.

Perhaps the World Champion fears Korchnoi's experience on both sides of the Grünfeld and therefore resorts to the defence he used against Karpov's 1 d4 in the 1984 and 1985 title clashes.

4 ♗f4!?

A curious idea, though it soon transposes into a known line. As in Korchnoi-Short, 'Viktor the Terrible' avoids 4 ♘f3 ♘f6 5 ♗g5 h6 6 bxf6, which is the currently fashionable continuation.

But one might have expected 4 cxd5 exd5 5 ♗f4 which Korchnoi used to win the most brilliant game of the 1981 World Championship v Karpov (5 ... c6 6 e3 ♗f5 7 g4 ♗e6 8 h3 Korchnoi-Karpov, Menas 1981, (13).

4	...	♘f6

5	e3	0-0
6	♖c1	c5

Kasparov gladly accepts an IQP in order to free his position.

7	dxc5	♗xc5
8	cxd5	exd5

9 ♘f3

Korchnoi is notorious for grabbing hot pawns, so why does he not go in for 9 ♘xd5? The reply 9 ... ♕a5+ is not convincing, nor is 9 ... ♘xd5 10 ♖xc5 ♘xf4 11 ♕xd8 ♘xg2+ 12 ♗xg2 ♖xd8 on account of 13 ♖xc8! ♖xc8 14 ♗xb7. Best is 9 ♘xd5 ♘xd5 10 ♖xc5 ♘xf4 11 ♕xd8 ♖xd8 12 exf4 ♗e6 13 a3 ♘c6 14 ♘f3 ♗b3 with sufficient lead in development to compensate for White's extra (doubled) pawn.

9	...	♘c6

10 ♗e2

The pawn snatch on d5 is even less convincing past move 9.

10 ...   ♗e6
11 0-0   ♖c8
12 ♘b5

White has some initiative but Kasparov defends actively.

12 ...   ♘e4
13 ♘d2

There are more long term prospects to be offered by 13 ♘bd4, accupying the traditional blockading square in front of the IQP.

13 ...   ♘xd2
14 ♕xd2   ♗b4
15 ♕d1   ♕b6
16 a3   ♗e7
17 b4   a5

Black's vigorous counter-attack forces White into a premature liquidation.

18 ♘d6   ♖cd8
19 ♘xb7

The only way to extricate the Knight. But this combination leads to no more than a draw.

19 ...   ♕xb7
20 b5

If Black's Knight moves then comes ♖c7. But White's play is easily parried.

20 ...   ♖c8!
21 bxc6   ♖xc6
22 ♖b1   ♖b6
23 ♖xb6   ♕xb6
24 ♗e5

Drawn. If anything, White still has a microscopic edge, since 24 ... ♗xa3 fails to 25 ♕a1! forking a3 and g7. However, objectively White cannot achieve anything tangible.

GAME TWENTY-ONE
NUNN-PORTISCH

1 e4 c5 2 ♘f3 d6 3 d4 cxd4 4 ♘xd4 ♘f6 5 ♘c3 a6 6 f4 e5 7 ♘f3 ♘bd7 8 a4 ♗e7 9 ♗d3 0-0 10 0-0 ♘c5 11 ♔h1 ♕c7 12 ♕e1 ♗e6 13 f5 ♗d7 14 g4 ♗c6 15 g5 ♘h5 16 f6 ♗d8 17 ♕h4 g6 18 ♗e3 ♘xd3 19 cxd3 ♔h8 20 ♘e2 d5 21 ♘g3 dxe4 22 dxe4 ♕d6 23 ♖ad1 ♕b4 24 ♘xe5 ♘xg3+ 25 hxg3 ♕xe4+ 26 ♕xe4 ♗xe4+ 27 ♔h2 ♗c7 28 ♗c5 ♗xe5 29 ♗xf8 ♖xf8 30 ♖fe1 ♗c2 31 ♖d2 ♗xa4 32 ♖xe5 h6 33 gxh6 ♔h7 34 g4 ♗xh6 35 g5+ ♔h7 36 ♖e4 ♗c6 37 ♖h4+ ♔g8 38 ♔g3 1:0

GAME TWENTY-ONE

NUNN - PORTISCH

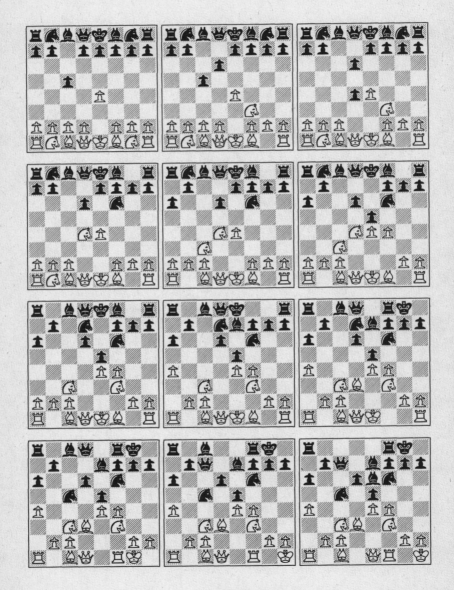

199

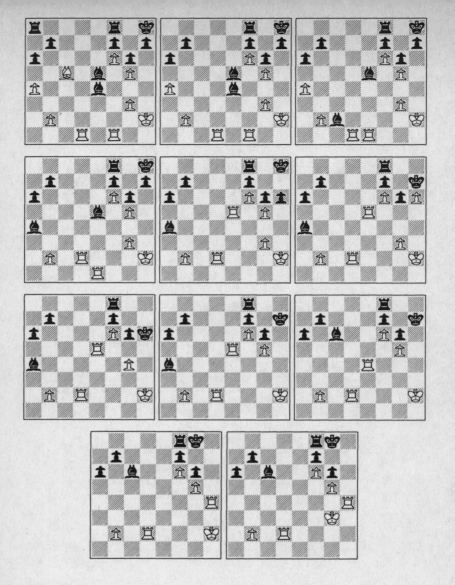

1:0

Nunn - Portisch

1	e4	c5
2	♘f3	d6
3	d4	cxd4
4	♘xd4	♘f6
5	♘c3	a6

Nunn is always stuck for choice against the Najdorf. He knows each variation so well and respects the opening so much that this early position is a real problem for him.

6	f4	e5

Black can omit e7-e5 altogether and switch to Dragon-like set ups with 6 ... ♛c7 and 7 ... g6 but White obtains some attack. Portisch counters in traditional Najdorf style.

7	♘f3	♘bd7
8	a4	

An indispensable part of White's plan. Before embarking on his kingside assault he prevents Black from gaining space with 8 ... b5. Since Black has not played ... ♛c7 8 ♗c4 also comes into consideration but then 8 ... b5 stands up well enough.

8	...	♗e7
9	♗d3	0-0
10	0-0	♘c5

Black can snatch a pawn here with 10 ... exf4 11 ♗xf4 ♛b6+ 12 ♔h1 ♛xb2 13 ♛e1 ♛b4 but Portisch is not willing, over the board, to defend such a position.

11	♔h1	

Either 11 ♛e1 or 11 ♛e2 have also been played but the text seems most economical, tucking the King into safety before revealing an attacking plan.

11	...	♛c7

Until now, 11 ... d5 was the accepted reply but recent games suggest that White gets an advantage, eg:

a) 12 fxe5 ♘fxe4 13 ♘d4! ♗g5 (13 ... f6) 14 ♕h5 ♗xc1 15 ♖axc1 g6 16 ♕h6 ♘xc3 17 bxc3 f5 18 exf6 ♖xf6 19 ♖xf6 ♕xf6 20 ♖f1 with an attack, Sax-Grünfeld Brussels 1985.

b) 12 ♘xe5 dxe4 (12 ... ♘fxe4 13 ♗xe4 dxe4 14 ♘d5! ♗e6 15 ♘xe7+ ♕xe7 16 f5 f6 17 ♘g4 ♗f7 and now 18 a5! was +− Nunn-King BRD 1986) 13 ♗e2 ♕c7 14 ♗e3 b6 15 ♕e1 ♗b7 16 ♕g3 ♘e6 17 ♖ad1 ♗c5 18 f5! +− Beliavsky-Chandler Vienna 1986.

12 ♕e1

Threatening 13 fxe5 dxe5 14 ♕g3.

12 ... ♗e6?!

Too provocative but Black may be worse here anyway, eg. 12 ... ♗d7 13 fxe5 dxe5 14 ♕g3 ♖e8 15 ♕xe5 ♗d6 16 ♕d4 ♘g4 17 ♘d5! and he doesn't have enough compensation for his pawn.

13 f5!

Why not. The White attack begins.

13 ... ♗d7
14 g4! ♗c6

14 ... ♘xg4 is out of the question with d5 and the g-file at White's mercy. Black's position disintegrates after 15 ♘d5 ♕d8 16 ♖g1 ♘f6 17 ♗h6 ♘e8 18 ♖xg7+ ♘xg7 19 ♕g3 ♗f6 20 ♖g1.

15 g5 ♘h5!

The only defence. Other moves allow f5-f6 and an invasion on the h-file.

16 f6 ♗d8
17 ♕h4 g6
18 ♗e3

White has a very strong position. For the time being Black has put paid to the kingside attack but he's very clogged up. Nunn points out the positional threat of 19 ♗xc5 dxc5 20 ♗c4 and therefore Black's Knight must move. Where to? 18 ... ♘e6 lines him up for 19 ♘d5 ♗xd5 20 exd5 ♘ef4 21 ♗xf4 exf4 (21 ... ♘xd4 22 ♕h6) 22 ♗f5! (intending 23 ♗g4) so Portisch has to make an undesirable exchange.

18 ... ♘xd3
19 cxd3 ♔h8!

Nunn thinks that this is Black's best defensive try. White is threatening ♘e2-g3 opening up the position and there's not a lot Black can do about it. Portisch can never

202

consider ♘xg3 at any point because of mate on the h-file so what he must do is to allow ♘xh5, and try to give up a pawn for some counter-play. After the game Portisch suggested 19 ... ♕d7!? as an alternative.

20 ♘e2   d5

A move which most of us would play, but in the circumstances it's not enough. Again 20 ... ♕d7 was the best try this time attacking the a4 pawn, eg. 21 ♘g3! (21 b3 ♕e6 22 ♖ab1 ♖c8 23 ♘g3 ♗d7 intending ♖c2, ♖c3) 21 ... ♗xa4 22 ♘xh5 gxh5 23 ♕xh5 ♗b5 24 ♖a3 but Black still has to defend against the threat of ♖g1-g4-h4.

21 ♘g3   dxe4

21 ... ♕d6 22 d4 + −

22 dxe4   ♕d6

23 ♖ad1

Beginning a tactical sequence leading to a winning position.

23 ...   ♕b4

23 ... ♕e6 24 ♗c5! ♖g8 25 ♗d6 leads to the loss of the e5 pawn. When this pawn falls Black's whole game will crumble. Thanks to his cornered King, he is still horribly gummed up.

24 ♘xe5   ♘xg3+

25 hxg3   ♕xe4+

If 25 ... ♗xe4+ 26 ♔g1 ♗b6 27 ♗xb6 ♕xb6 28 ♖f2 and the twin threats of ♕xe4 and ♕h6 are impossible to meet.

26 ♕xe4   ♗xe4+

27 ♔h2

Threatening 28 ♗c5. Neither 27 ... ♔g8 28 ♗c5 ♖e8 29 ♘xf7! ♔xf7 30 ♖d7+ ♔e6 31 f7 ♖f8 32 ♖d4 ♖xf7 33 ♖d6+ nor 27 ... ♖c8 28 ♖d7 ♔g8 29 ♘g4 helps out so ...

27 ...   ♗c7

28 ♗c5!

Refuting Black's play.

28 ...   ♗xe5

29 ♗xf8   ♖xf8

30 ♖fe1

Black's back rank is too

weak to allow any real compensation now.

30 ... ♗c2
31 ♖d2 ♗xa4

If 31 ... ♗xg3 32 ♔xg3 ♗xa4 White's Rook enters triumphantly with 33 ♖e7 and gobbles up the pawns.

32 ♖xe5 h6

What else? The stranglehold is too great.

33 gxh6 ♔h7
34 g4 ♔xh6
35 g5 + ♔h7
36 ♖e4 ♗c6
37 ♖h4 + ♔g8
38 ♔g3

It's all over. White doubles on the h-file and mates.

1:0

Portisch, Nunn, Martin.

OFF THE BOARD

Back in the hotel restaurant, Portisch — who does not eat lamb — had difficulty conveying this adequately to the Belgian waiter. Finally, comprehension dawned and the offending dish was removed to the accompaniment of a muttered remark about the difficulty pleasing Muslims.

"Doubtless very difficult", thought Portisch. "Especially if the hotel waiters cannot differentiate between lamb and pork".

Another unhappy diner was John Nunn, who has an aversion to seafood. After this was pointed out, a shrimp cocktail was removed to be replaced by the soup course.

However, before the first waiter could return with the soup, a second spotted empty white tablecloth and helpfully deposited another shrimp cocktail before the Englishman.

This too disappeared and, none too soon for the now ravenous Nunn, the soup course finally arrived. It was minestrone. Shrimp-flavoured minestrone.

ROUND EIGHT

Game No.22	Short	0:1	Nunn
Game No.23	Portisch	0:1	Korchnoi
Game No.24	Kasparov	1:0	Hübner

Short-Nunn and Kasparov-Hübner went the usual way of games between these opponents, though Short had to blunder away a winning position to fall victim to an ingenious swindle. Kasparov crushed Hübner in similar style to Hübner's own win the previous day against Short. For once, Korchnoi managed to overcome Portisch, though his position from the opening had looked most unconvincing.

SCORES: Kasparov 6; Korchnoi, Short & Nunn 4; Hübner 3½; Portisch 2½

So with two rounds to spare, the world champion was assured of at least a share of first prize. The tournament had already become a contest only for second place.

GAME TWENTY-TWO
SHORT-NUNN

1 e4 e5 2 ♘f3 ♘c6 3 ♗b5 a6 4 ♗a4 ♘f6 5
0-0 ♗e7 6 ♖e1 b5 7 ♗b3 0-0 8 c3 d5 9 ed
♘xd5 10 ♘xe5 ♘xe5 11 ♖xe5 c6 12 d4 ♗d6
13 ♖e2 ♕h4 14 g3 ♕h5 15 ♘d2 ♗h3 16 f3
♗c7 17 a4 b4 18 c4 ♘f6 19 ♘e4 ♕g6 20 ♘f2
♗f5 21 ♗c2 ♖fe8 22 ♗xf5 ♕xf5 23 ♖xe8+
♖xe8 24 ♕g2 ♖d8 25 ♗e3 ♗b6 26 ♔b3
♗xd4 27 ♖d1 c5 28 ♗xd4 cxd4 29 ♕xb4
♕d7 30 ♕b6 h5 31 ♕xa6 ♖b8 32 ♖d2 h4
33 ♕a5 ♖b3 34 ♕c5 ♕b7 35 ♖d3 h3+ 36
♔xh3 ♖xd3 37 ♘xd3 ♕xf3 38 ♕xd4 ♕f1+
39 ♔h4 ♕f5 0:1

GAME TWENTY-TWO

SHORT-NUNN

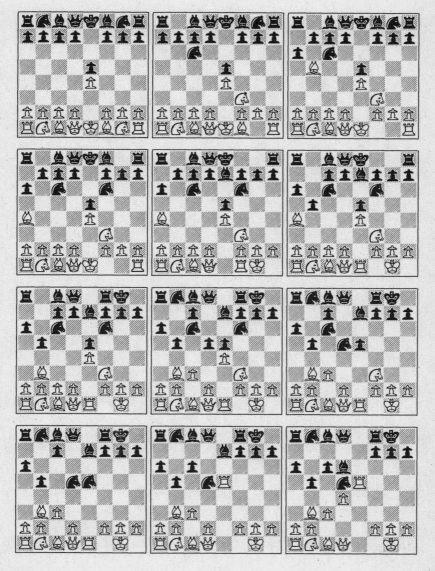

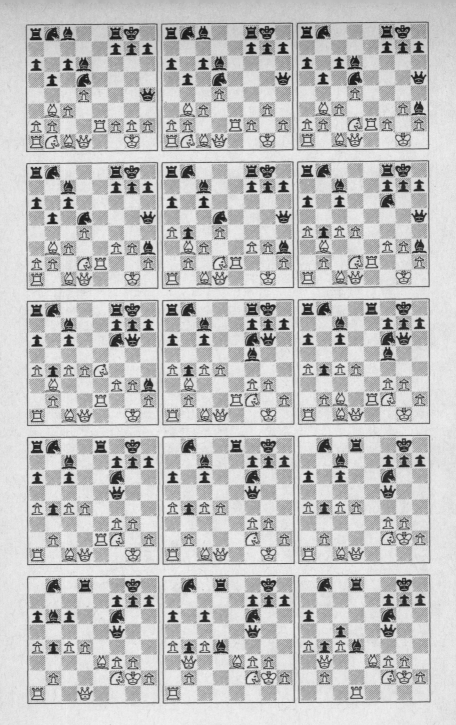

0:1

Short - Nunn

1	e4	e5	
2	♘f3	♘c6	
3	♗b5	a6	
4	♗a4	♘f6	
5	0-0	♗e7	
6	♖e1	b5	
7	♗b3	0-0	
8	c3	d5	
9	exd5	♘xd5	
10	♘xe5	♘xe5	
11	♖xe5	c6	
12	d4	♗d6	
13	♖e2!?		

The first point of interest in this very well tried and tested variation. Short is trying to find a defensive function for his Rook to perform but it can be exposed on e2.

13 ... ♕h4

13 ... ♗g4 was possible, forcing 14 f3 ♗h5 15 ♗xd5 cxd5 when Black has two active Bishops in compensation for his minus pawn.

14	g3	♕h5	
15	♘d2	♗h3	

Regaining material with 15 ... ♗g4 leaves White with a superior ending after 16 f3 ♗xf3 17 ♘xf3 ♕xf3 18 ♕f1 ♕xf1+ 19 ♔xf1. Retreats of the Queen after 18 ... ♕h5 are still worse, eg. 19 ♗d2 and with 20 ♖ae1 to come, White is excellently coordinated.

16	f3	♗c7	

16 ... f5 17 c4 + −

17	a4	b4	
18	c4	♘f6	

Supposedly theoretically equal but ...

19	♘e4!		

19 ... ♕g6

The alternatives were unappetizing, eg:

a) 19 ... ♕xf3 20 ♘g5 ♕h5 21 ♘xh3 ♕xh3 22 ♗g5! + − White has two strong Bishops and all the play.

b) 19 ... ♘xe4 20 ♖xe4
♗f5 21 ♖e7! ♗d6 22 ♖e3!
+– Black doesn't have
much for a pawn any more.

20 ♘f2   ♗f5
20 ... ♗xg3? 21 ♘xh3 +–
21 ♗c2   ♖fe8
22 ♗xf5   ♕xf5
23 ♖xe8+   ♖xe8
24 ♔g2   ♖d8
25 ♗e3   ♘b6

Judicious exchanges have
increased White's advantage
to winning proportions.
Nigel now returns a pawn
temporarily to activate his
Queen.

26 ♕b3

26 ...   ♗xd4
27 ♖d1   c5
28 ♗xd4   cxd4
29 ♕xb4   ♕d7
30 ♕b6   h5

A last desperate thrust.

31 ♕xa6
31 h4! +–
31 ...   ♖b8
32 ♖d2   h4
33 ♕a5   ♖b3
34 ♕c5   ♕b7
35 ♖d3??

Not 35 ♘d3 when ♘e4! is
unclear but 35 ♕f5! was
comfortable enough. A
disorientated Nigel Short
now gets blown away.

35 ...   h3+
36 ♔xh3   ♖xd3
37 ♘xd3   ♕xf3
38 ♕xd4??

It even took a further ?? to
lose this game. After 38 ♘f4!
♘e4 White only draws but
this is preferable to what
happens.

38 ...   ♕f1+
39 ♔h4   ♕f5

0:1

GAME TWENTY-THREE
PORTISCH-KORCHNOI

1 d4 Nf6 2 c4 g6 3 g3 Bg7 4 Nf3 0-0 5 Bg2 d6 6 Nc3 Nc6 7 0-0 Bf5 8 Re1 Qc8 9 e4 Bh3 10 Nc2 Bxg2 11 Kxg2 e5 12 d5 Ne7 13 Ne1 Nd7 14 Nd3 a5 15 Bg5 f6 16 Be3 b6 17 f4 f5 18 Qe2 Qa6 19 Nb5 fe 20 Nf2 Nf5 21 Rac1 Qb7 22 fe Nxe5 23 Bf4 e3 24 Bxe5 Bxe5 25 Nd3 Rae8 26 Nxe5 Rxe5 27 g4 c6 28 dc Qxc6+ 29 Kh3 Ng7 30 Rxf8+ Kxf8 31 Rf1+ Kg8 32 Nd4 Qe4 33 Qf3 Qxf3+ 34 Nxf3 Re4 35 b3 Ne6 36 Kg3 g5 37 Re1 h6 38 h4 Kg7 39 hg hg 40 Rd1 e2 41 Re1 Kf6 42 Nd2 Re5 43 Nf3 Re4 44 Nd2 Re5 45 Nf3 Nf4 46 Rh1 Nd3 0:1

GAME TWENTY-THREE
PORTISCH - KORCHNOI

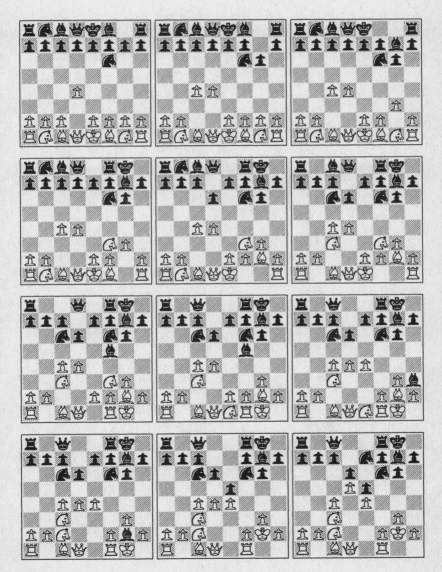

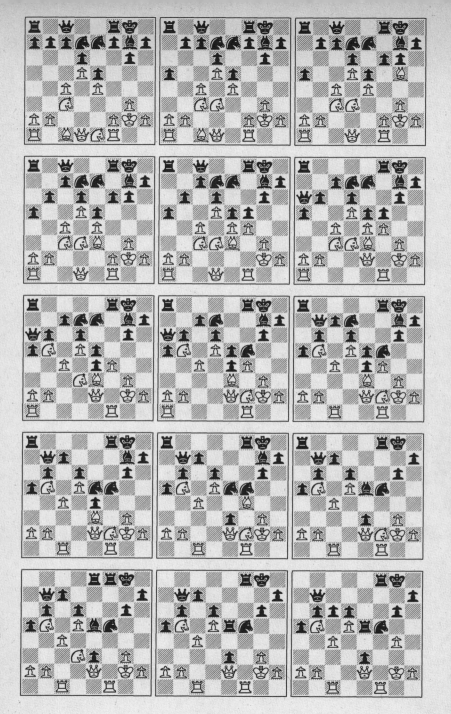

214

215

0:1

1	d4	♘f6	14	♘d3	a5
2	c4	g6	15	♗g5	

Trying to provoke a weakness on e6. White has the initiative.

3	g3	♗g7	15	...	f6
4	♘f3	0-0	16	♗e3	

16 ♗d2!?

5	♗g2	d6	16	...	b6
6	♘c3	♘c6	17	f4	

17 f3

7	0-0	♗f5	17	...	f5
8	♘e1				

If 17 ... ♘c5 then 18 ♘xc5 bxc5 19 fxe5! fxe5 20 ♖xf8+ gives White the better game.

I also played this move against Tal in our 1965 Candidates Match.

18 ♕e2?

8	...	♕c8
9	e4	♗h3
10	♘c2	♗xg2
11	♔xg2	

White has some advantage in space but Black has adequate chances.

11	...	e5
12	d5	♘e7

It will be difficult for Black to begin a kingside attack without his white squared Bishop.

13	♘e1	♘d7

Here I made a mistake. 18 ♕d2 was more accurate protecting the Knight on c3 and Korchnoi would not have as many chances as in the game. For example 18 ♕d2! ♕a6 19 b3 fxe4 20 ♘xe4 exf4 21 ♘xf4 ♗xa1 22 ♖xa1 and despite White's loss of the exchange his Knights are dominantly placed.

18 ...   ♕a6!
19 ♘b5

The difference becomes apparent. White cannot play 19 b3.

19 ...   fxe4
20 ♘f2   ♘f5
21 ♖ac1?

Maybe 21 ♖ae1 was better, but not 21 ♘xc7 ♕xc4!

21 ...   ♕b7
22 fxe5   ♘xe5

In contrast to an earlier variation it is now the Black Knights which dominate.

23 ♗f4   e3
24 ♗xe5   ♗xe5

If 24 ... exf2 25 ♗xg7 ♖ae8! 26 ♕d2 ♘e3+ 27 ♕xe3! ♖xe3 28 ♗x8 ♔xf8 29 ♖xf2 with an unclear position.

25 ♘d3   ♖ae8
26 ♘xe5   ♖xe5
27 g4   c6!!

An excellent move with both players approaching time trouble.

28 dxc6   ♕xc6+
29 ♔h3   ♘g7
30 ♖xf8+   ♔xf8
31 ♖f1+   ♔g8
32 ♘d4   ♕e4
33 ♕f3   ♕xf3+
34 ♘xf3   ♖e4
35 b3   ♘e6
36 ♔g3   g5

It is hopeless for White — Black's advanced pawn is too strong.

37 ♖e1   h6
38 h4   ♔g7
39 hxg5   hxg5
40 ♖d1   e2
41 ♖e1   ♔f6
42 ♘d2   ♖e5
43 ♘f3   ♖e4
44 ♘d2   ♖e5
45 ♘f3   ♘f4!

If now 46 ♘xe5 ♔xe5 47 ♔f3 ♔d4 the Black King settled on d2 and ♘d3 then follows. White runs out of moves.

46 ♖h1   ♘d3

0:1   Portisch.

218

GAME TWENTY-FOUR
KASPAROV-HÜBNER

1 d4 d5 2 c4 c6 3 ♘c3 ♘f6 4 e6 e6 5 ♘f3
♘bd7 6 ♗d3 ♗b4 7 a3 ♗d6 8 e4 dxe4 9
♘xe4 ♘xe4 10 ♗xe4 e5 11 0-0 0-0 12 ♗c2
♖e8 13 ♖e1 exd4 14 ♖xe8+ ♕xe8 15 ♕xd4
♗e7 16 ♗g5 ♗xg5 17 ♘xg5 ♘f6 18 ♖d1
♗e6 19 ♖e1 ♕d8 20 ♘xe6 fxe6 21 ♕e3
♔h8 22 h3 ♕d7 23 g4 ♖e8 24 ♕e5 ♕d8 25
♔g2 ♕b6 26 ♖d1 c5 27 ♗a4 ♖f8 28 ♖d6
♕c7 29 ♖xc6 ♕f7 30 ♕xc5 ♘xg4 31 ♕xf8+
♕xf8 32 hxg4 1:0

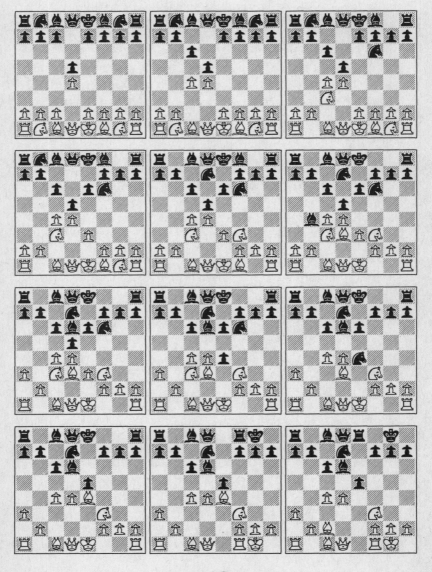

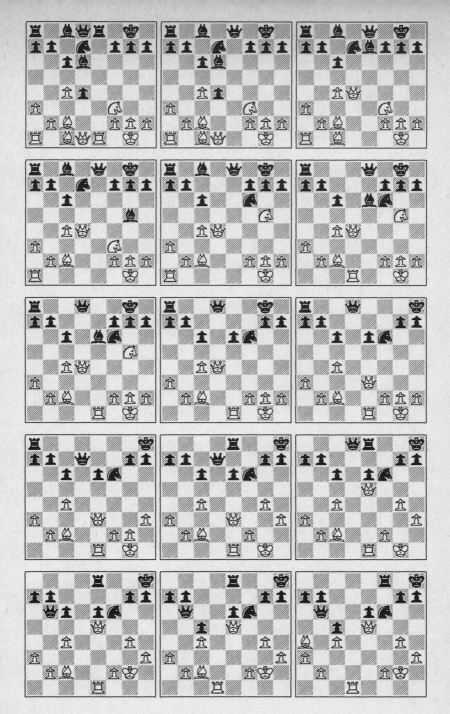

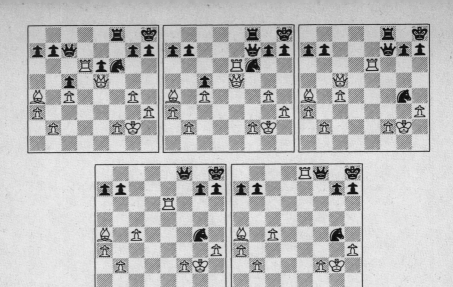

1:0

Kasparov - Hübner

1	d4	d5
2	c4	c6
3	♘c3	♘f6
4	e3	e6
5	♘f3	♘bd7
6	♗d3	♗b4!?

Romih's variation, which more or less disappeared from GM praxis after Botvinnik inflicted a very nasty defeat on former World Champion Euwe in the 1948 World Championship Match Tournament.

Since then, improvements have been unearthed for Black, but Romih's invention never caught the imagination.

7	a3	♗d6

Black has just wasted a tempo (White's move a3) so why did he not simply play 6 ... ♗d6? We shall soon see.

8	e4	dxe4
9	♘xe4	♘xe4
10	♗xe4	e5
11	0-0	0-0

White can now win a clear pawn with 12 dxe5 ♘xe5 13 ♘xe5 ♗xe5 14 ♗xh7+ (14 ♕h5 f5) 14 ... ♔xh7 15 ♕h5+ ♔g8 16 ♕xe5, but after 16 ... ♕d3 White cannot win. One major factor is the opposite Bishop syndrome; this, taken with White's severe weakness on b3 leaves Black with no losing prospects.

If Black had, however, not provoked 7 a3 to create this weakness, then White could torture Black for ages with his extra pawn.

12	♗c2!	

Simple and strong. White keeps his advantage by exploiting his lead in development. The White Queen will centralise by recapturing on d4. Such small, but deadly accurate moves, are frequently to be found in Kasparov's play. They are essential to maintain an opening edge with White against a top-match opponent.

12	...	♖e8
13	♖e1	exd4
14	♖xe8+	♕xe8
15	♕xd4	♗e7

A surprising but correct retreat. 15 ... ♗c5 leads to difficulties after 16 ♕d3 ♘f8

17 b4! to be followed by ♗b2 and ♖e1. Hübner now plans ♗e7-f6.

16	♗g5	♗xg5
17	♘xg5	♘f6
18	♖d1	

Although Kasparov's dynamic style is usually compared with Alekhine's he has maintained White's opening advantage here with the crystal clarity and simplicity of Capablanca. In spite of the balanced pawn structure, White's pieces are generally more active, and he dominates the d-file.

18 ... ♗e6

This looks like a fatal positional blunder, but more obvious moves also fail, viz: 18 ... h6 19 ♘e4! ♘xe4 20 ♕xe4 (threatening ♕xe8+ and ♕h7+) 20 ... ♕xe4 21 ♖d8+ ♔h7 22 ♗xe4+ g6 23 ♗f5 winning; alternatively 18 ... ♗d7 19 ♘e4! (threatening ♘xf6+ and ♘d6) 19 ... ♘xe4 20 ♕xd7 with decisive penetration.

18 ... ♗g4!? 19 ♘xh7 seems good for White but it may have been Hübner's best chance. Black gets active after 19 ... ♘xh7 20 ♕xg4 ♘xg5 21 ♕xg5 ♕e2 and with only major pieces left this is precisely what he needs.

19	♖e1	♕d8
20	♘xe6	fxe6
21	♕e3	♔h8

Black is positionally crushed as a result of the superiority of White's Bishop over Black's Knight, and also Black's very weak e-pawn on the open file. It is, However, extraordinarily instructive to observe how the World Champion encompasses the destruction of the Black position without permitting a shred of counterplay.

Here, for example, Hübner could struggle somewhat after the precipitate 22 ♕xe6 ♕d4! Kasparov prefers to prepare a deadly advance of his g-pawn.

22	h3	♕d7
23	g4	♖e8
24	♕e5	♕d8
25	♔g2	♕b6
26	♖d1	

Black is being reduced to utter helplessness by White's trans-board constriction strategy. In a situation when there is no good defence to White's threat of g5 plus ♖d7 or g5 plus b4, c5 and

♖d4-h4, Hübner sheds material.

26	...	c5
27	♗a4	♖f8
28	♖d6	♕c7
29	♖xe6	♕f7

Hoping for a swindle in the f-file ...

30 ♕xc5!

Exploiting the attack on f8 to net a second pawn.

30	...	♘xg4
31	♕xf8 + !	

... the trapper trapped. White lands the f-file coup himself and wins a piece.

31	...	♕xf8
32	hxg4	

1:0. ♖e8 is unstoppable.

KASPAROV-HÜBNER   Rd 8

— Kasparov's TV commentary

1	d4	d5
2	c4	c6
3	♘c3	♘f6
4	e3	e6
5	♘f3	♘bd7
6	♗d3	♗b4

KASPAROV: He likes this very old system, ♗b4 instead of ♗d6 or dxc4. He lost in the first round against Korchnoi after 7 a3 ♗a5, and in my opinion this position should be better for White. I saw the Encyclopaedia today and I have prepared something very interesting.

7	a3	♗d6

KASPAROV: He came back on d6. The difference is that he knows the pawn on a3 should be worse for White in one very important position. Now I should play e4. I think he's going to sacrifice a pawn and play the position without a pawn, but with good chances for a draw. I can explain this decision because my score against Hübner is plus five, five losses for him. Of course he dreams about a draw in this game. But I can play without risk.

8	e4	dxe4
9	♘xe4	♘xe4
10	♗xe4	e5
11	0-0	0-0

KASPAROV: This is the point of Black's idea. Now I think Hübner expects 12 dxe5 ♘xe5 13 ♘xe5 ♗xe5 14 ♗xh7+ ♔xh7 15 ♕h5+ ♔g8 16 ♕xe5 and now ♕d3. This is very important; there is no move b3 to protect the pawn on c4. It gives very good chances for a draw. I want to keep as many pieces on the board as possible. Traditionally 12 ♗c2 should be best; he plays 12 ... ♖e8, I play 13 ♖e1 and after 13 ... exd4 14 ♖xe8+ ♕xe8 15 ♕xd4 I'm better. It's no great advantage for me, but there's no choice. I don't like to play the position with an extra pawn and small chances to win.

12	♗c2	♖e8
13	♖e1	exd4
14	♖xe8+	♕xe8
15	♕xd4	♗e7

KASPAROV: Oh, Hübner has made a very strong move. Now I should find something very strong because in one move, after ♘f8, Black is okay, with no weakness. I can't give him time to have a bishop on f6. I should develop my pieces. 16

226

Bg5 is a strong move. If he takes 16 ... Bxg5 then 17 Nxg5 Nf6 and I have a very strong move 18 Rd1. Then if he plays 18 ... Bg4 19 Bxh7+, or 18 ... h6 19 Ne4 Nxe4 20 Qxe4 Qxe4 21 Rd8+ is winning, or if he plays 18 ... Be6 then 19 Re1. Okay, 16 Bg5 should be better for me. If he takes 16 ... Bxg5 17 Nxg5 then 17 ... Nf8, I can play 18 Ne4 then into d6. It's a very good position for my knight.

16	Bg5	Bxg5
17	Nxg5	Nf6
18	Rd1	Be6

KASPAROV: Hübner spent a lot of time to find this move because he doesn't like to play the position without a pawn in the ending after 18 ... Bg4 19 Bxh7+ Nxh7 20 Qxg4 Nxg5 21 Qxg5 Qe2 22 Qc1, but I think that would have been better for him. Now I just play 19 Re1 and I can't see a move for Black, because if 19 ... Qd7 20 Bxh7+ Nxh7 21 Nxe6 with an extra pawn and a completely winning endgame.

19	Re1	Qd8
20	Nxe6	fxe6
21	Qe3	Kh8

KASPAROV: I don't like now to take this pawn on e6, because of Qd4 with counterplay on the black squares. I must find the plan to beat Black. I think it's too difficult if I win the pawn on e6, for example 22 h3 Qd7 23 Re2 e5 24 Qc3 Qd4 25 Rxe5 Qxc3 26 bxc3 Re8. It's an extra pawn in the endgame but I'm not sure whether it's winning. Well, once in this game I have refused to take his pawn, maybe I should do it against just to keep him under pressure. My queen will come to e5, then maybe h3 and g4 or g3. I don't know, g4 is very good, then Rd1. I can use this d-line. Okay, it's very difficult for Black, he has no active counterplay at all.

22	h3	Qd7
23	g4	Re8
24	Qe5	

KASPAROV: It's a great pleasure to see this position, with all my pieces so strong. I can play Re2 and Kg2. I think Hübner is very unhappy now. He can do nothing except wait for my active moves.

23	...	Qd8
25	Kg2	Qb6

KASPAROV: Now after 26 Rd1 I'm winning easily because I cut his queen off on one side, and I have many threats. If he plays 26 ... Rf8, I play Rd2 and then b4. He has no moves at all.

26	Rd1	c5

KASPAROV: Now I should

choose between ♖d6 and ♗a4. What's better. What's the difference. This is winning. That is winning too. Okay ♗a4 is stronger, then ♖d6 and take this pawn on e6.

27	♗a4	♖f8
28	♖d6	♕c7
29	♖xc6	♕f7

KASPAROV: Now I can play f4, I can play ♕f5. Oh, I can take 30 ♕xc5 and if 30 ... ♘xe4, I take 31 ♕xf8+

♕xf8 32 ♖e8 ♕xe8 33 ♗xe8 ♘d6 gives some chances to him. Oh I can take on f8: 31 ♕xf8+ ♕xf8 then 32 ♖xe4 is the simplest. He has no defence to ♖e8. If 32 ... b5 33 ♗xb5 ♕a8+ 34 f3 and no defence again. 30 - ♕xc5 ♘xg4 is the same. Okay, I have two extra pawns.

30	♕xc5	♘xg4
31	♕xf8+	♕xf8
32	hxg4	1:0

ROUND NINE:

Game No.25	Kasparov	1:0	Short
Game No.26	Hübner	1:0	Portisch
Game No.27	Korchnoi	½:½	Nunn

Kasparov exacted revenge upon Nigel Short in a most impressive fashion. After allowing a combination (19 ♘e6) to break open the position, Short seemed happy that the liquidations had led only to equality, but suddenly, after 25 ♗c2, Black found himself in a lost position. The drastic collapse of Short's game seemed to come as a surprise as much to Kasparov as to the Englishman.

Meanwhile, Hübner was taking advantage of the luckless Portisch, and Korchnoi seemed to be enjoying himself at Nunn's expense until, after missing several apparently winning continuations, he let his opponent escape with a draw.

SCORES: Kasparov 7; Korchnoi, Hübner & Nunn 4½; Short 4; Portisch 2½.

GAME TWENTY-FIVE
KASPAROV-SHORT

1 d4 e6 2 ♘f3 ♘f6 3 c4 d5 4 ♘c3 ♗e7 5 ♗g5 h6 6 ♗xf6 ♗xf6 7 e3 0-0 8 ♖c1 c6 9 ♗d3 ♘d7 10 0-0 dc 11 ♗xc4 e5 12 h3 ed 13 ed ♘b6 14 ♗b3 ♗f5 15 ♖e1 ♗g5 16 ♖a1 ♘d7 17 d5 ♖c8 18 ♘d4 ♗g6 19 ♘e6 fe 20 de ♔h7 21 ♕xd7 ♕b6 22 e7 ♖fe8 23 ♕g4 ♕c5 24 ♘e4 ♕xe7 25 ♗c2 ♖f8 26 g3 ♕d8 27 ♖ad1 ♕a5 28 h4 ♗e7 29 ♘c3 ♗xc2 30 ♖xe7 ♖g8 31 ♖dd7 ♗f5 32 ♖xg7+ ♔h8 33 ♕d4 1:0

GAME TWENTY-FIVE

KASPAROV-SHORT

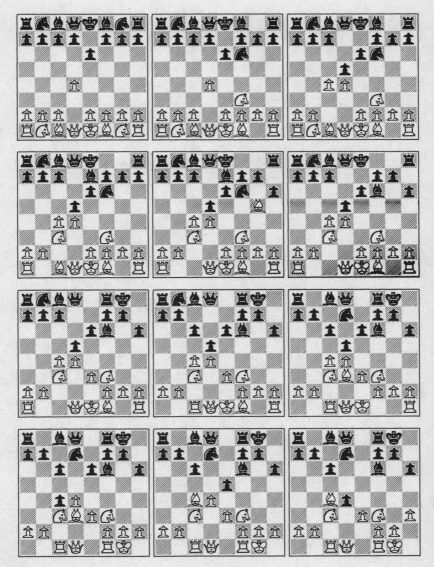

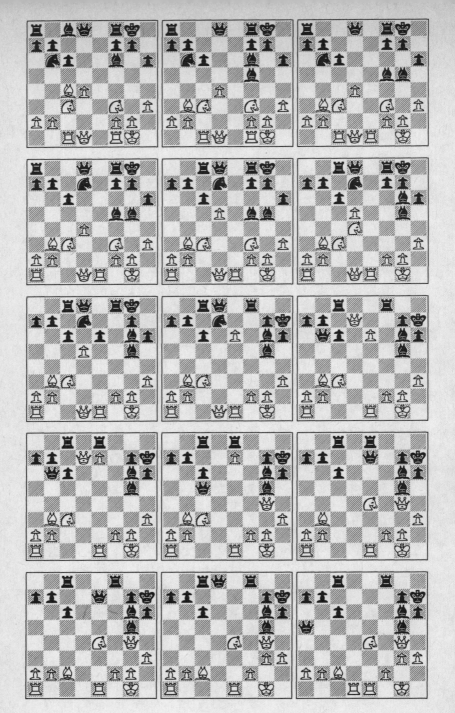

232

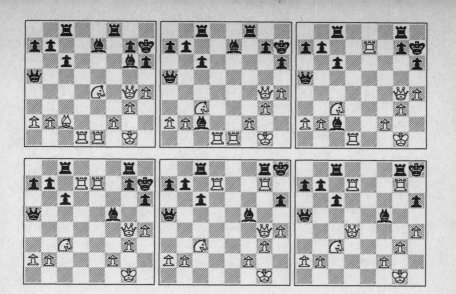

1:0

Kasparov - Short

1	d4	e6
2	♘f3	♘f6
3	c4	d5
4	♘c3	♗e7
5	♗g5	h6
6	♗xf6	♗xf6
7	e3	0-0
8	♖c1	c6
9	♗d3	♘d7
10	0-0	dxc4
11	♗xc4	e5
12	h3	exd4
13	exd4	♘b6
14	♗b3	♗f5

This is a funny position. Black has two Bishops, no weaknesses, and an isolated pawn on d4 to attack. Against this White has better control of the centre and some pressure against f7. But if you compare the pieces, you will see that almost all of the White pieces are superior to their Black counterparts. This naturally leads us to the conclusion that White can improve his position more easily than Black and move quickly too. A good example of this comes from the 22nd game in the Kasparov-Karpov match, eg. ♖e1 a5 16 a3 ♖e8 17 ♖xe8+ ♕xe8 18 ♕d2 ♘d7 19 ♕f4! ♗g6 20 h4 += and because of White's active Queen Karpov's position was very difficult to play. Perhaps a better approach was seen in Rashkovsky-Beliavsky USSR Championship 1986 where Black played 15 ♖e1 ♕d7 16 ♕d2 a5 17 a3 a4 18 ♗a2 ♖fe8 19 ♕f4 ♗e6 20 ♗xe6 ♖xe6 21 ♖xe6 ♕xe6 22 ♕c7 ♕b3. There is no obligation to take on e8 with the Queen but my impression is that White can improve somewhere along the line. Short agrees and plays an improvement of his own.

15	♖e1	♗g5
16	♖a1	

16 ♘xg5 ♕xg5 can't give anything for White because Black now has such a good square for his Queen.

16	...	♘d7

To protect the e5 square. On 16 ... ♘d5, then 17 ♖e5! is good.

17 d5! ♖c8?!

Kasparov suggests that the best try for Black was 17 ... ♘c5 intending after 18 dxc6 just to play 18 ... bxc6. The further 19 ♕xd8 ♖axd8 20 ♘xg5 hxg5 21 ♖e5 ♘xb3 22 axb3 does not give any advantage. Against 17 ... ♘c5 he intended 18 ♗c2! and the further 18 ... ♗xc2 19 ♕xc2 cxd5 20 ♖ad1 is actively + −. He thinks that after 17 ... ♖c8 Black is just trying to maintain his position and defend it but remarkably, this natural move is a mistake.

18 ♘d4!

Better than 18 dxc6 bxc6 19 ♘d4 ♗g6 when a lot of Black's tension has been released.

18 ... ♗g6
19 ♘e6!!

Bang! Out of an apparently clear sky comes a move which disrupts the Black position. Suddenly Short is fighting just to stay on the board.

19 ... fxe6
20 dxe6 ♔h7

Black must get his King off the back rank. eg. 20 ... ♔h8?? 21 exd7 ♖c7 22 ♕d6! ♗f5 23 ♕xf8+ ♕xf8 24 ♖e8 + −.

21 ♕xd7 ♕b6

21 ♕xd7 22 exd7 just brings the White pawn closer to touchdown, eg. 22 ... ♖cd8 23 ♖ad1 ♗f5 24 ♗e6 and Black cannot round it up. Short wriggles for a while but the advanced pawn has the value of an extra piece.

22 e7

Kasparov is not disturbed by the threat on f2 in the slightest. If Black takes he's had it. eg. 22 ... ♕xf2+ 23 ♔h1 ♖fe8 24 ♘e4! ♗xe4 25 ♖xe4. What can be done here?

22 ... ♖fe8
23 ♕g4!

A new menace appears on the horizon. The World Champion sees that the advanced pawn will not win the game on its own and hastens to embarrass the Black minor pieces. White threatens h4-h5. By the time Short is in a position to take on e7 he will have been mated.

23 ...♕c5

23 ... ♖c7 wins the pawn but loses the game. eg. 24 h4! ♖cxe7 15 ♖xe7 ♗xe7 26 h5!-

♗d3 27 ♖d1. White drives the Bishop off the h7-b1 diagonal, gives check on c2 — Queen in to g6, next game please.

24   ♘e4

24 h4 ♗f5! and when the White Queen moves Black takes on e7. If 24 ♗e6 then simply 24 ... ♖a8 and White doesn't achieve anything.

24   ...   ♕xe7

25   ♗c2!!

Kasparov really wants revenge for his earlier defeat. He has surrendered his advanced pawn but in return the Black pieces are all exposed. White's horrible threat is 26 f4 and 27 ♘g5+, winning the Black Queen.

25   ...   ♖f8

26   g3

A remarkable follow up. White renews the threat of f2-f4.

26   ...   ♕d8

27   ♖ad1

There will be no further mercy in this game. Black is

lost.

27   ...   ♕a5

28   h4!   ♗e7

28 ... ♗f5 29 ♘xg5+ hxg5 30 ♕xg5 threatens 31 ♖e7

29   ♘c3

When you hit Kasparov on top form every one of his moves seems like a sledge-hammer blow. Both White Rooks appear on the seventh rank and what remains of the Black position is swept away like debris in a rushing torrent.

29   ...   ♗xc2

30   ♖xe7   ♖g8

31   ♖dd7

31   ...   ♗f5

32   ♖xg7+   ♔h8

33   ♕d4   1:0

Kasparov, Martin.

KASPAROV-SHORT

— The Players TV commentaries

1 d4 e6 2 ♘f3 ♘f6 3 c4 d5 4 ♘c3 ♗e7 5 ♗g5 h6 6 ♗xf6 ♗xf6 7 e3 0-0 8 ♖c1 c6 9 ♗d3 ♘d7 10 0-0 dxc4 11 ♗xc4 e5 12 h3 exd4 13 exd4 ♘b6 14 ♗b3 ♗f5

KASPAROV: I like to play this position when I'm White. It looks equal because Black has two bishops and no weakness in the position, but anyway White keeps control of the central squares and can keep Black under pressure for a long time. I have played this position, but anyway White keeps control of the central squares and can keep Black under ressure for a long time. I have played this position with White many times and with very good results. Even Karpov couldn't make a draw in our last match. Now 15 ♖e1 is of course the best move, but I don't know what Nigel specially prepared for this game.

15 ♖e1

SHORT· Well, so far so good. At least I had this position on my set this morning. My idea is simply to play 15 ... ♗g5. Then if he takes 16 ♘xg5 I simply recapture with my queen and the position is simplified a bit. I'd be threatening his h-pawn and if he moves his queen I play ♖e8 with no big difficulties for me. I suppose he could play ♖a1, but if that's his idea then surely this is a good idea for me.

15 ... ♗g5

KASPAROV: Now I can take on g5, but as far as I remember, it's not so clear. It gives good counterplay to Black with his queen on g5 or g6. I should play ♖a1. It looks strange but anyway ♗g5 is strange too and I keep it under pressure with my knight. My knight can take this bishop or go to e5, then ♕f3 and pressure on f7. I think ♖a1 is best. There is no difference between c1 and a1.

16 ♖a1

SHORT: I'll continue with my play to neutralise his play by sticking my knight on d7. This prevents ♖e5 and it's not clear to me how he'll improve his game. After 16 ... ♘d7 17 ♘e4 I play ♗f4 and he has no way of improving his position. He can easily become worse here if he's not careful.

16 ... ♘d7

KASPAROV: Of course he protects the very important square e5, but he took control from the d5 square. It means I should play d5, but he can play ♘c5 and if I take on c6 it gives me nothing. But after 17 d5 ♘c5 I can play 18 ♗c2 ♗xc2 19 ♕c2 cxd5 20 ♖ad1. Maybe it's a big advantage. Anyway it's better for me. I can play without any risk.

17 d5

SHORT: I guess this was the only critical line. I really couldn't imagine what else he was going to come up with. But still it's not too worrying. Well, he's intending to take on c6 and to play ♘d4 winning a pawn. I'd like just to defend this pawn with ♖c8 and if he takes I recapture with the pawn. He has another possibility though after 17 ... ♖c8, that's 18 ♘d4. I guess after 18 ♘d4 ♗g6 he has some tricky moves. He can take on c6, I recapture, then ♘e6, then I take, ♗xe6+, ♖f7, so no problem. But what if he plays 18 ♘d4 ♗g6 then 19 ♘e6 immediately. My goodness! 19 ... fxe6 20 dxe6 ♔h7 21 exd7 ♖c7. It's very difficult but actually I have to analyse it. If I make some mistake here, then maybe I'm just losing. Well, if I get this pawn back, which I

appear to be doing, then not only am I equalising, I'm making an immediate draw, because he would have no chances to increase the pressure. Well, he could also play 21 ♕xd7, but then I have ♕b6. Very difficult position, but it feels as though I'm all right here. Let's give it a go.

17 ...   ♖c8

KASPAROV: That's an unexpected move. It's very strange, something should happen on the d5-a8 diagonal, or on the a2-g8 one. I feel something will happen very soon. I should use this d-pawn. 18 ♘d4 ♗g6 19 ♘e6, very interesting, to know if he really saw this move. Okay 18 ♘d4 ♗g6 19 ♘e6 fxe6 20 dxe6 ♔h7. I can choose between 21 exd7 or ♕xd7. I will choose late. I feel that ♘d4 is my best chance.

18 ♘d4   ♗g6
19 ♘e6   fxe6
20 dxe6   ♔h7

KASPAROV: Now if 21 exd7 ♖c7 22 ♗e6 ♗f5 24 ♕c2 g6. Oh, I overlooked this first move before. It may be slightly better for me, but it's not enough. Now if I take this knight with the queen 21 ♕xd7 ♕xd7 22 exd7 ♖cd8 23 ♗e6 ♗f5 24 ♖ad1 ♗xe6 25 ♖xe6 ♖f7 26 ♖ed6, it should be winning. So 21

♕xd7 ♕b6 or ♕f6. Or he plays maybe 21 ... ♗h4. Then I can play 22 g3 or even take on d8: 22 ♕xd8 ♗xf2+ 23 ♔f1 ♖cxd8 24 e7 ♗d3+ 25 ♘e2 ♗b6 mate, but 25 ♖e2 ♗xe2+ 26 ♘xe2 and I have an extra piece. Very good for me. And 21 ♕xd7 ♕b6 I should play 22 e7 and if 22 ... ♖xf2 23 ♘a4 wins, or 22 ... ♕xf2+ 23 ♔h1 ♖fe8 24 ♘e4 looks like a completely winning position.

21 ♕xd7   ♕b6
22 e7

SHORT: Two moves to consider here. Let's have a brief look at this: 22 ... ♕xf2+ 23 ♔h1 ♖fe8 then he goes 24 ♘e4. This looks disastrous. I can't afford to give up my bishop. Also I want my queen to support this ♖c7 move. Well, I don't see how he hangs onto his pawn at e7 and, well, what's he going to do to me?

**   ...   ♖fe8**

KASPAROV: That was another unexpected move. Black's position looks very suspicious but I can't immediately see the best move. He's trying to take this pawn, the pride of my position. I must do something immediately. I think that the most important weakness in the black position is the bishop on g6 and the white squares. I can't use my pieces to attack this bishop. The only chance is to use the h-pawn. It looks like my game gainst Karpov, I tried to use this pawn in the 22nd game to attack this bishop and then to arrange to create a very strong attack on the white squares on the kingside. Okay, now if I play 23 ♕g4, for example, 23 ... ♖c7 24 h4 ♖xe7 25 ♖xe7 ♗xe7is nothing too, of course. I should put my queen on the kingside and arrange the attack.

23 ♕g4

SHORT: He's intending h4 and h5 and then developing some very nasty threats along the b1-h7 diagonal. But I still have ♕c5 which is very nice. If 24 h4, I simply play ♗f5.

25 ...   ♕c5

KASPAROV: Now I can play 24 ♗e6 ♖c7 25 ♘e4 ♕xe7 26 f4. It's much better for me. But if he plays 24 ♗e6 ♖a8 or ♖b8 - a8 is better - what ca I do. It's just a slight advantage in the endgame after ♘e4. I don't like it. Something should happen. Okay, this is the idea. I can use this b1-h7 diagonal. 24 ♘e6 ♕xe7 25 ♗c2. And how can he save his piece on g6. The threat is f4. Very simple. Or h4. The threat is f4 and ♘g5+. It's a very funny position.

24 ♘e4   ♛xe7

KASPAROV: Now ♝c2. Yes, there's no defence. Very strange position. I can't believe my eyes but it looks like I'm winning a piece.

25 ♝c2

SHORT: That is quite unpleasant. It looks like such an innocuous move, but I totally underestimated this. He has some threats of simply f4. Well f4 is just winning a piece. I just absolutely did not understand this idea ♝c2. It looks like a defensive ove, but what can I play? I think I'm completely lost. Well, he's threatening f4, so let's stop that at least.

25 ...   ♖f8

KASPAROV: He protects f4, but now I can win a piece after 26 h4 ♝xh4 27 g3 ♝g5 28 f4, but I can just improve my position. If I play 26 g3 what can he do. 26 ... ♖c8 27 h4 ♝d2, well there's 28 ♛xg6+ and 29 ♘xd2+. It's completely winning. Or 26 g3 ♝f5 27 ♘d6, beautiful! No, I can't reject such a beautiful move as ♘d6. I should play g3 and it's like *Zugzwang* on the whole

board.

26 g3

SHORT: I'm surprised because h4 won by force there. Well I just have to keep playing moves and hope the knock-out doesn't come. Get my queen off the e-file.

26 ...   ♛d8
27 ♖ad1   ♛a5
28 h4   ♝e7

KASPAROV: Maybe now even ♘f6+, but it's not necessary. 29 ♘d6 ♝xc2 30 ♖xe7 ♖g8 31 ♘c8, oh, I don't want to calculate it all. 29 ♘c5 is not so clear. Okay, play 29 ♘c3 ♝xc2 30 ♖xe7 ♖g8 31 ♖dd7. There's no defence. After 31 ... ♝g6 32 ♛d4 mates.

29 ♘c3   ♝xc2
30 ♖xe7   ♖g8
31 ♖dd7

SHORT: Well, I should resign now, in fact I should have resigned a few moves ago. But I'll just play one or two more to try and get it up to a respectable number.

31 ...♝f5
32 ♖xg7+ ♔h8
33 ♛d4
1:0

GAME TWENTY-SIX

HÜBNER · PORTISCH

1 e4 e5 2 ♘f3 ♘c6 3 ♗b5 a6 4 ♗a4 ♘f6
5 0-0 ♗e7 6 ♖e1 b5 7 ♗b3 d6 8 c3 0-0 9 h3
♗b7 10 d4 ♖e8 11 ♘bd2 ♗f8 12 a4 ♛d7
13 d5 ♘e7 14 c4 ♘g6 15 ♗c2 c6 16 b3 b4
17 ♘h2 ♛c7 18 ♘g4 ♗e7 19 ♘f1 cd 20 cd
♘xg4 21 hg ♗c8 22 ♘e3 ♗g5 23 ♘f5 ♗xc1
24 ♖xc1 ♛d8 25 ♗d3 ♘e7 26 ♛d2 ♖b8
27 ♖c2 ♘xf5 28 gf f6 29 ♖ec1 ♖e7 30 ♖c6
♖a7 31 ♛e2 a5 32 ♗b5 ♗b7 33 ♖c7 ♖c8
34 ♛c4 ♖aa8 35 f3 ♚f8 36 ♚f2 ♖ab8
37 ♛e3 g6 38 ♗d7 ♖xc7 39 ♛xc7 ♛xc7
40 ♖xc7 ♗a6 41 ♗e6 ♖b7 42 ♖c6 ♗f1
43 ♖xd6 ♗c4 44 ♖d8+ 1:0

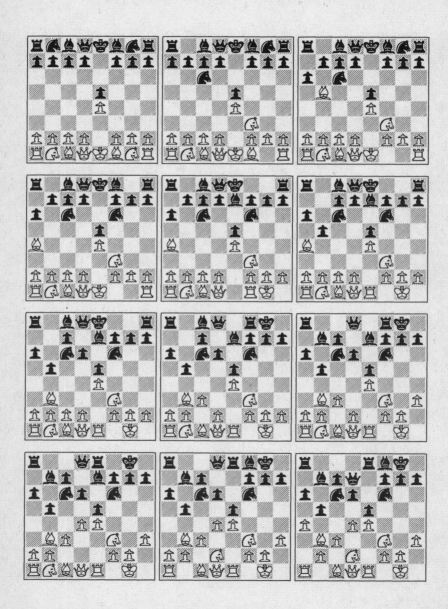

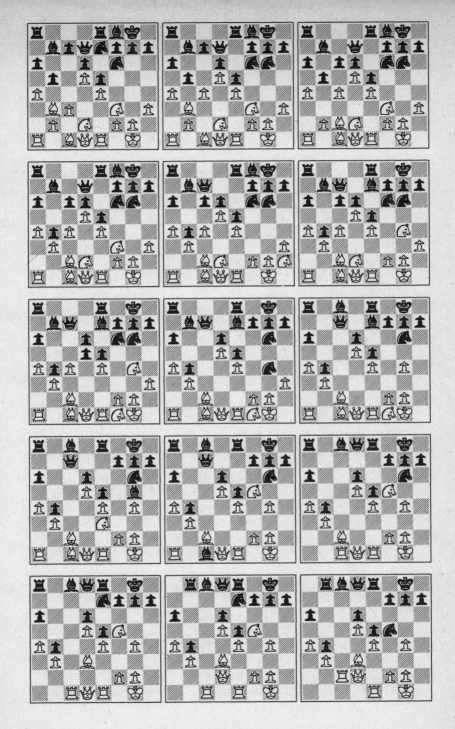

243

244

1:0

Portisch in play against Short (round 6).

245

Hübner · Portisch

1	e4	e5	
2	♘f3	♘c6	
3	♗b5	a6	
4	♗a4	♘f6	
5	0-0	♗e7	
6	♖e1	b5	
7	♗b3	d6	
8	c3	0-0	
9	h3	♗b7	
10	d4	♖e8	
11	♘bd2	♗f8	
12	a4	♛d7	

The current fashionable Zaitsev variation. It became popular during the three Kasparov-Karpov matches, and Karpov relies on it as his main defence to 1 e4. To me it seems excessively passive.

13	d5	♘e7
14	c4	

White's play is logical and powerful. With this move he establishes a Q-side initiative where the situation is still fluid. But on the K-side White also has a plus — a static space advantage. In fact, Portisch drifts into a lost position without really committing any serious error.

14 ...♘g6

Perhaps this is too congested. Maybe 14 ... g6!?

15	♗c2	c6
16	b3	b4

A reasonable decision since Black can hardly consider exchanging on a4 or c4.

17	♘h2	♛c7
18	♘g4	♗e7
19	♘f1	cxd5?

This is probably the decisive strategic error, although it appears natural enough to open the c-file while White is building up on the King's wing. In fact, Black should either maintain the tension or play 19 ... c5, entirely blocking the Queen's flank, and then slog out a purely defensive battle on the other side of the board. Black's problem now is that his Q-side pawns are weak, and it is White who gains control of the all-important c-file.

20	cxd5	♘xg4
21	hxg4	♗c8

Otherwise the Black QB is biting on granite on b7.

22	♘e3	♗g5

Another natural move, since Black's KB is restricted by its own centre pawns, but the prospective Bishop exchange enhances White's domination of the only open file.

23	♘f5	♗xc1
24	♖xc1	♕d8
25	♗d3	♘e7
26	♕d2	♖b8
27	♖c2	

Black's pawns on a6 and b4 are under fire. Meanwhile Hübner simply and efficiently trebles his major pieces in this c-file. Portisch has to perform painful contortions with his rooks to avoid immediate disaster.

27	...	♘xf5
28	gxf5	f6
29	♖ec1	♖e7
30	♖c6	♖a7
31	♕e2	a5

Another horrible concession. Now White's Bishop has full rein to penetrate via the Q-side light squares.

32	♗b5!	♗b7
33	♖c7	♖c8
34	♕c4	♖aa8
35	f3	♔f8
36	♔f2	

Hübner centralises his King while Black is utterly helpless.

| 36 | ... | ♖ab8 |
| 37 | ♔e3 | g6 |

Losing at once, but there is, in case case, no good defence to ♗d7.

38	♗d7!	♖xc7
39	♕xc7	♕xc7
40	♖xc7	♗a6
41	♗e6	♖b7
42	♖c6	♗f1
43	♖xd6	♗c4
44	♖d8+	

Resigns. If 44 ... ♔g7 45 d6 wins, or 44 ... ♔e7 45 ♖h8.

Hübner's best games, and this is one of them, exhibit all the forceful logic and panache of his illustrious compatriot, Dr Tarrasch at his most resplendent.

GAME TWENTY-SEVEN

KORCHNOI - NUNN

1 d4 g6 2 e4 d6 3 c3 Nf6 4 Bd3 Bg7 5 Nf3
0-0 6 0-0 c5 7 dc dc 8 h3 Nc6 9 Qe2 Qc7 10
Re1 Nd7 11 Bc2 b6 12 a4 Bb7 13 Nbd2
Rad8 14 Nf1 Qc8 15 Bg5 Ba6 16 Qe3
Qb7 17 Rad1 c4 18 Nd4 Nde5 19 Nb5 Na5
20 Qe2 Bxb5 21 ab Qc7 22 f4 Nd3 23
Bxd3 cd 24 Rxd3 h6 25 Bh4 Rxd3 26
Qxd3 Rd8 27 Qe2 Qxf4 28 Bxe7 Re8 29
Bb4 Nb7 30 Qf3 Qe5 31 Ne3 Qxb5 32
Rf1 Qd7 33 Nd5 Nc5 34 Bxc5 bc 35 Rd1
Qb7 36 Rd2 Qc6 37 Rf2 Qd7 38 Qf4 Re5
39 Rd2 Qe6 40 Nc7 Qe7 41 Nd5 Qe6 42
Nc7 Qe7 43 Nd5 Qe6 ½:½

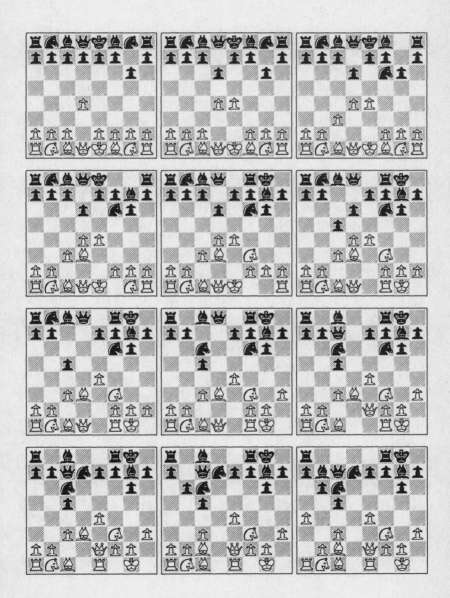

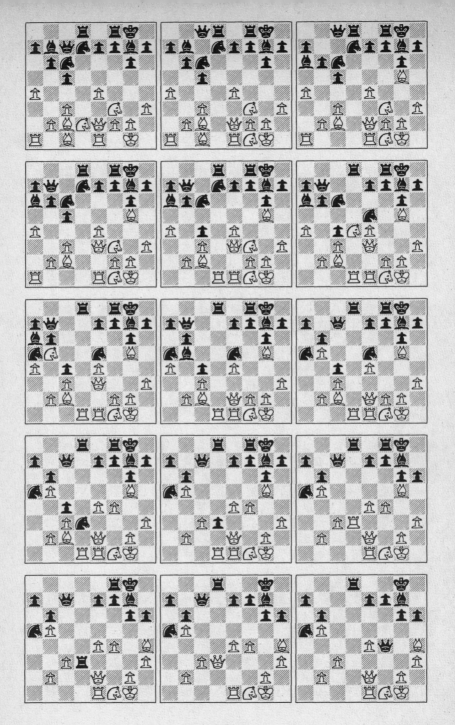

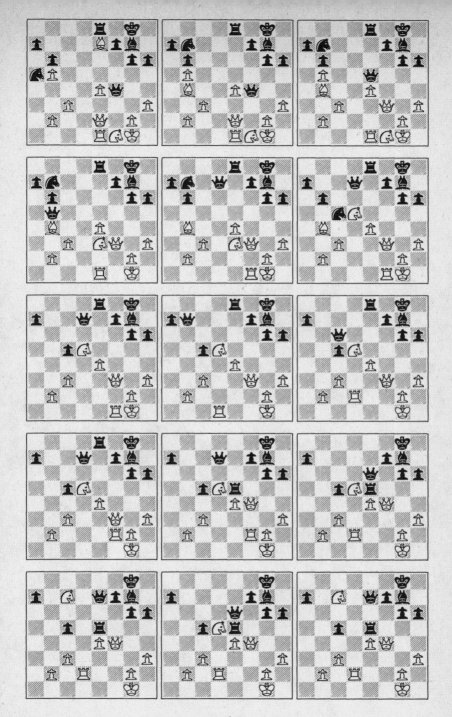

½:½

After the game Nunn and Korchnoi, together with Short, helping analysis in the B-tournament.

Korchnoi - Nunn

1	d4	g6	
2	e4	d6	
3	c3	♘f6	
4	♗d3	♗g7	
5	♘f3		

5 f4 is also a serious test of Black's resources. The move order adopted by Korchnoi is, in fact, recommended in John Nunn's own book, 'The Pirc for The Tournament Player'.

5	...	0-0
6	0-0	c5!?

As Nunn points out in his monograph, 6 ... ♘c6 7 d5! is unsatisfactory for Black, whether he reacts with ... ♘b8 or allows ... ♘e5 8 ♘xe5 dxe5 9 c4. Nunn proposes 6 ... a5 while I have tried 6 ... ♘h5!? to be followed by ... e5 and perhaps arduous equality. I have now come to the conclusion that 6 ... c5 is best, fighting to increase the radius of activity of Black's KB.

7	dxc5	dxc5
8	h3	♘c6

It is generally believed that such positions favour White, especially if he can play e5 to blot out Black's KB. Nunn now struggles fiercely against just this eventuality.

9	♕e2	♕c7
10	♖e1	♘d7!

Not 10 ... ♘h5 11 e5!

11	♗c2	b6
12	a4	♗b7
13	♘bd2	

Maybe 13 ♘a3!?

13	...	♖ad8
14	♘f1	♕c8
15	♗g5	

Setting up pressure against e7 and tempting Black to weaken himself with ... h6 ... g5, etc..

15	...	♗a6
16	♕e3	♕b7
17	♖ad1	c4!

It is not in Nunn's active nature to sit idly by and be positionally squashed by moves like ♘g3 and ♗h6. With this thrust Nunn secures possible out-posts for his Knights on b3 and d3, and substantially distracts White from his own plans.

18	♘d4	♘de5
19	♘b5	♘a5
20	♕e2	♗xb5
21	axb5	♕c7
22	f4	♘d3

The crisis. Black offers a pawn to activate his pieces. At this stage he has no choice, but the idea had to be enlisted when Nunn committed himself to 17 ... c4!

23	♗xd3	cxd3
24	♖xd3	h6
25	♗h4	

25 ♖xd8 ♖xd8 26 ♗h4 ♕xf4 is a direct transposition.

25	...	♖xd3
26	♕xd3	♖d8
27	♕e2	

If he tries to cling to the f4 pawn White must reckon with ... ♘c4 and ... ♕c5+.

27	...	♕xf4
28	♗xe7	♖e8
29	♗b4	♘b7
30	♕f3	

White trades his 'b5' pawn which is already very weak, for some attacking prospects in the f-file.

30	...	♕e5
31	♘e3	♕xb5
32	♖f1	♕d7
33	♘d5	♘c5
34	♗xc5	bxc5
35	♖d1	♕b7
36	♖d2	♕c6
37	♖f2	♕d7
38	♕f4!?	

It would have been more prudent to repeat at once with 38 ♖d2 =. In any case, the position stays balanced.

38	...	♖e5
39	♖d2	♕e6
40	♘c7	♕e7
41	♘d5	

Now White acquieses.

41	...	♕e6

254

42 ♘c7 ♛e7
42 ... ♛c4 43 ♖d8+ ♚h7
44 ♖d7 with a sufficient

counterattack against f7.

43 ♘d5 ♛e6
Drawn.

*Korchnoi thinks while Hübner
writes down his move.*

KORCHNOI · NUNN   Rd 9

— The Players TV commentaries

1	d4	g6
2	e4	d6
3	c3	♘f6
4	♗d3	♗g7
5	♘f3	0-0
6	0-0	c5
7	dxc5	dxc5
8	h3	♘c6
9	♕e2	♕c7
10	♖e1	♘d7
11	♗c2	b6
12	a4	♗b7
13	♘bd2	♖ad8

KORCHNOI: Two moves ago, with my advantage in space and superiority in the centre I had the better game. Now, when I move my knight from d2, I allow him counterplay on the white squares c4, d3 and so on. This I feel will happen. So, in this position I have only one way, to go ♘f1 and eventually to e3 and d5.

14 ♘f1

NUNN: I'd really like to try and make something of those weak squares he's got on the queenside. Perhaps I could play ♘a5 followed by c4 and ♘c5 with the threat to invade on b3 or d3. But I don't want to move the knight on c6 away from the centre at the moment. If I stick it on a5 for several

moves, it looks as though I might have to suffer some accident with e5 or ♗g5. Yes, I think the knight ought to stay in the centre. How then can I get hold of those squares on the queenside? I could improve the position of my bishop by playing ♕c8 and ♗a6. Then I could play perhaps c4, ♘c5 or ♘a5 or ♘e5 as appropriate. The bishop definitely appears to be better placed on a6 than on b7.

14	...	♕c8
15	♗g5	♗a6
16	♕e3	

NUNN: His move ♗g5 puts me in an awkward position. I can't play ♘e5 now, because he just exchanges and if I take back with the knight, which is what I want to do, the pawn on e7 is undefended. For the same reason I can't play ♘a5. It certainly looks very committal to play c4 right away, but perhaps I should do that. On the other hand, I can defend the pawn on e7 and then move the knight. But which piece should I defend it with? If I defend it with the rook by playing ♖e8, then after a subsequent exchange of rooks on the d-file, my defensive rook is going to be deflected. So I probably ought to use the queen. Yes, if I play ♕b7 after which I move the knight away, the queen will defend the pawn.

16 ... ♕b7

KORCHNOI: This is strange. What is that? Well, I have always known he doesn't understand chess. What's he doing with his pieces? Well, he had to play f6 to cut off my bishop, and then to move ♘e5, ♘a5 and c4. Oh it's a relief. My move is obvious. I continue to develop my queenside.

17 ♖ad1 c4

KORCHNOI: So c4. It's a new lemon. He allows me to occupy the square d4. Now I have so many good moves. First of all, what the heck - Kasparov would play like this: 18 b4 cxb3 19 ♗xb3, then ♗g5 then ♘d4. Well, it's a little bit risky. Kasparov is Kasparov, I have my own style. Let's see, what about e5? Whether it works or not. It's a pawn sacrifice. Again, let's leave it to Kasparov. My move is quite obvious, ♘d4.

18 ♘d4

NUNN: That's unexpected and again an awkward move. If I play 18 ... ♘de5, he can play 19 ♘xc6. I don't want to take back with the knight, he just plays f4. If I take back with the queen, though, he can take on d8 and take on e7 winning a pawn. Oh this is starting to look really unpleasant. If I take on d4, he takes back with the c-pawn and I don't have any squares at all for my pieces. What on earth can I do here? I've also got to worry about ♘b5, I suddenly notice. But the immediate threat is to win the e-pawn. Perhaps I can play 18 ... ♘de5 after all. If he takes 19 ♘xe5 ♕xe5 he wins the pawn, but I get my knight to d3. Yes, the knight will be very active there. I think that will be worth a pawn, or even if it isn't I don't think I've got any better alternative.

18 ... ♘de5

KORCHNOI: Again I have two possibilities. One is 19 ♘xc6, if 19 ... ♘xc6 then I play f4 with a good advantage. If he takes 19 ... ♕xc6 20 ♗xe7 ♖xd1 21 ♖xd1 ♖e8 22 ♗a3 ♘d3 23 ♘d2, threatening 24 ♘xe4 winning. Well, instead of 22 ... ♘d3, he has perhaps the move 22 ... f4 which looks a little bit dangerous. Black has some compensation because of the awkward positions of some white pieces. Aha, I have a normal move, ♘b5.

19 ♘b5

NUNN: I'm not seeing any

of his moves today at all. I expected him to take on c6, but he's played something completely different. Now he's going to play f4, driving my knight from its central position and forcing me right back on the defensive. I've got to be ready to answer f4 with ♘d3. At the moment it just loses a pawn, but I can prepare it with 19 ... ♘a5, then 20 f4 ♘d3, 21 ♗xd3 cxd3 22 ♖xd3 ♘c4, followed by 23 ... ♖xd3 and ♘xb2, I get my pawn back.

19	...	♘a5
20	♕e2	♗xb5
21	axb5	♕c7
22	f4	♘d3
23	♗xd3	cxd3
24	♖xd3	

NUNN: I now see that I made a bit of a miscalculation. I'd intended to get my pawn back by playing 24 ... f6 25 ♗h4 ♕xf4, but now I see that by continuing 26 ♗g3 ♕g5 27 b4 ♘b7 28 h4, my queen gets driven back to the disgusting square h6. And then would come something like ♖a1 and my pawn on a7 is suffering a rather dreadful fate indeed. So 1 have just lost a pawn. Well, nothing to do about that, I just have to play on. I can exchange the f4 pawn for e7. That must be a good idea because it leaves him with a weak pawn. So I'll play h6.

24	...	h6
25	♗h4	♖xd3
26	♕xd3	♖d8
27	♕e2	♕xf4
28	♗xe7	♖e8
29	♗b4	♘b7

KORCHNOI: So, some problems. My pawns on b5 and e4 are weak. The only square I can defend both pawns with the queen is e2, but it's not a good square because of the confrontation of queen and rook on the e-file. I'll try to improve the position of my pieces with ♕f3. I want an ending here.

30 ♕f3

NUNN: That's a slightly peculiar move. I didn't expect that. Well, I can attack a pawn now. It's my greatest achievement so far.

30 ... ♕e5

KORCHNOI: Well, I don't want to defend the pawn. I play ♘e3. He cannot take on e4 because of ♘c2.

31 ♘e3

NUNN: All his moves are unexpected. I'm sure he ought to be playing ♖a1 at almost any move here and getting this pawn on a7. Instead, he seems to be just giving me this pawn on b5. Well now I just have to bank on his time-trouble. He's obviously got something prepared, but we'll just have to wait and see what it is.

31 ... ♕xb5

KORCHNOI: Oh damn! Instead of ♘e3, ♖a1 was winning on the spot. In that position he was dead lost after ♖a1. What the hell was I doing? But still I have something. I have ♖f1, or ♘d5. What's first? I don't have much time. Okay ♖f1.

32   ♖f1

KORCHNOI: Mamma mia! ♘d5 was winning easily. After 32 ♘d5 ♛d7 33 ♖d1 wins on the spot!

NUNN: Well again all his moves are unexpected, but rather more pleasantly so than before. I was really worried about ♘d5. But now my move's forced, I must defend f7.

32	...	♛d7
33	♘d5	♘c5
34	♗xc5	bxc5

KORCHNOI: I have to consider my failure. I failed to win this fantastic position. Well at least I have to keep equilibrium here. I'm a little bit worse. My pawn on e4 is weak.

35   ♖d1   ♛b7

36	♖d2	♛c6
37	♖f2	♛d7
38	♛f4	♖e5
39	♖d2	♛e6
40	♘c7	

NUNN: Well, I can force a draw here by playing ♛e7. He has to go back to d5 and I simply return to e6. But I wonder if it's possible for me to play for a win by playing ♛c4. There's no obvious way for him to defend the pawn on e4. He could perhaps try 41 ♖d8+ and 42 ♖d7, but then I have the nasty trick ♖f5 and that must be a winning position for me. But I think perhaps 40 ... ♛c4 41 ♖d8+ ♔h7 42 ♘d5. Yes, that's really nasty. He stops my ♖f5 trick and if I take the pawn on e4 with either queen or rook, then ♘f6+ comes. In fact, I would be in danger of losing. So I should probably go back.

40	...	♛e7
41	♘d5	♛e6
42	♘c7	♛e7
43	♘d5	♛e6

½:½

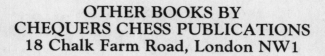

OTHER BOOKS BY
CHEQUERS CHESS PUBLICATIONS
18 Chalk Farm Road, London NW1

The Book of the World Championship
Kasparov v. Karpov
London/Leningrad 1986
Wade, Miles, Bronstein, Hartston,
Blackstock, Martin, Lancaster, Thomas
£9.95 softback, £14.50 hardback

The Game of the Round
Dubai Olympiad 1986
Wade, Martin, Smyslov, Averbakh,
Gufeld, Lancaster, Blackstock
£9.95 softback

ROUND TEN:

Game No.28	Short	0:1	Korchnoi
Game No.29	Portisch	½:½	Kasparov
Game No.30	Nunn	½:½	Hübner

A slightly anti-climactic last round after the fine excitement of the earlier play in the tournament. Kasparov, who had felt very tired even at the start of the event, was happy to give Portisch his first half-point since round four. Nunn and Hübner had a fairly level game throughout, so the excitement was left to Korchnoi, with a fighting effort to secure second prize. Short was simply not in the right mood to put up much resistance.

FINAL SCORES:
Kasparov 7½;
Korchnoi 5½;
Nunn & Hübner 5;
Short 4;
Portisch 3.

GAME TWENTY-EIGHT

SHORT - KORCHNOI

1 e4 e6 2 d4 d5 3 ♘c3 ♗b4 4 e5 c5 5 a3
♗xc3+ 6 bc ♘e7 7 ♘f3 ♕a5 8 ♗d2 ♘bc6
9 ♗e2 cd 10 cd ♕a4 11 ♗e3 b6 12 ♕d3 ♘b4
13 ♕b5+ ♕xb5 14 ♗xb5+ ♘bc6 15 ♗d2
♗d7 16 ♗a6 f6 17 ef gf 18 ♗c3 h5 19 ♘h4
♔f7 20 0-0 ♖ag8 21 f4 ♖g4 22 g3 ♖xh4 23
gh ♘f5 24 ♔f2 ♘cxd4 25 ♗xd4 ♘xd4 26 c4
♘b3 27 ♖ad1 ♘c5 28 ♗b5 ♗xb5 29 cb ♔g6
30 ♖g1+ ♔f5 31 ♔e3 ♖c8 32 ♖g7 ♘b3 33
♖d3 d4+ 34 ♔f3 ♖c3 35 ♖xc3 dc 36 ♖c7
c2 0:1

GAME TWENTY-EIGHT
SHORT - KORCHNOI

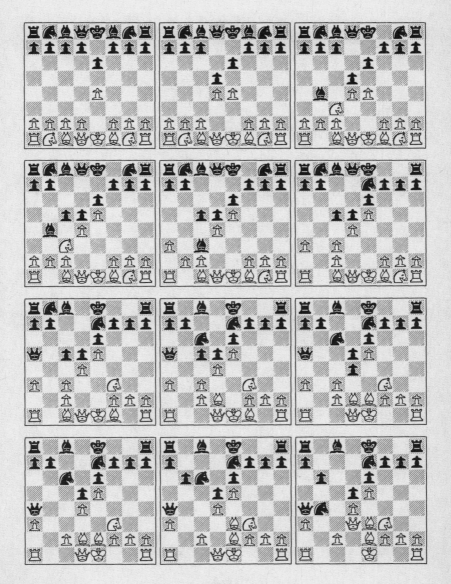

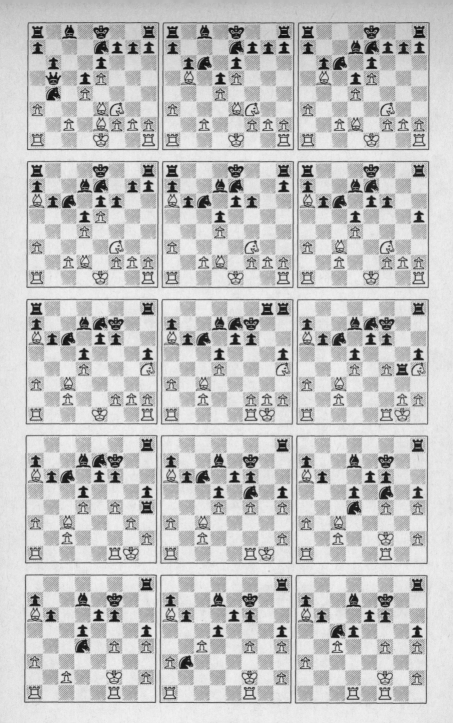

264

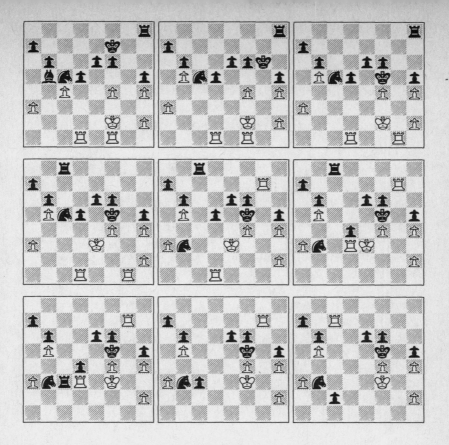

0:1

Short · Korchnoi

1	e4	e6
2	d4	d5
3	♘c3	♗b4
4	e5	

Ljubojević had scored a notable triumph with 4 a3 versus Korchnoi at Tilburg a month or so prior to this event. Short opts for the traditional approach.

4	...	c5
5	a3	♗xc3+
6	bxc3	♘e7
7	♘f3	♕a5

Korchnoi varies from his game with Nunn where 7 ... ♗d7 was played.

8	♗d2	♘bc6
9	♗e2	cxd4
10	cxd4	♕a4
11	♗e3?!	

A curious square for White's QB in the Winawer-Nimzovitsch variation. More normal would be 11 ♗c3.

11	...	b6

Korchnoi prepares to exchange off Black's QB, so often the problem piece of Black's entire defence strategy. Short takes immediate steps to prevent its deployment at a6.

12	♕d3	♘b4

13	♕b5+?	

After this unwarranted exchange White has nothing. It may have been repugnant to Short to admit it, but White has no more than equality, which can be demonstrated by 13 ♕d1! ♘bc6 14 ♕d3 =, in fact, inciting a repetition. In this, 13 ... ♘xc2+ 14 ♔d2 ♕a5+ 15 ♔xc2 ♗d7 16 ♔b2 is hopelessly unsound for Black.

13	...	♕xb5
14	♗xb5+	♘bc6

Black is obliged to retreat, but White's minor pieces are not left on well co-ordinated squares.

15	♗d2	

And now the White QB is rerouted to c3. The idea is to

stop Black pushing forward in the centre with ... e5.

15 ...   ♗d7

Threatening the trick ... ♞xe5.

16 ♗a6

In any case, in principle White does not wish to have his KB face Black's QB. The exchange of light-squared Bishops would leave White with Knight plus inferior Bishop (hemmed in by dark-squared pawns) against Black's Knight pair. Also, White's back-ward c2 pawn, exposed on the open file, looks even weaker if light-squared bishops go.

If Black now heads for a draw with 16 ... ♗c8 — hoping for 17 ♗b5 ♗d7 18 ♗a6 = White side-steps with 17 ♗d3! In that case, Black must lose a tempo to play ... ♖c8 (stopping this is another idea behind 16 ♗a6). However, by this stage Korchnoi was not thinking of a draw. A win would push him forward in this final round to clear second place, a wonderful performance for the veteran of the tournament.

16 ...   f6

17 exf6

This gives Black a potentially mobile central pawn majority, and cedes him the open g-file.

Both of these factors come to assume tremendous importance.

But if White does not exchange on f6, Black's ... fxe5 will saddle White with a weak pawn on e5.

17 ...   gxf6

18 ♗c3   h5

19 ♞h4   ♔f7

20 0-0?

Planning f4 and f5. Short can have had not the slightest inkling of the brilliant plan Korchnoi now proceeds to implement. Had he dreamt of what was in Korchnoi's mind he would have played 20 f4 ♖ag8 21 ♗d3 making doubly sure that the Black KN can be exchanged if it goes to f5.

20 ...   ♖ag8

21 f4

All in the interests of clamping down on ... e5, and blocking the lateral radius of activity of Black's QR should it rest on g4.

21 ...   ♖g4

22 g3   ♖xh4!!

An unexpected and impressive exchange sacrifice, exploiting his control of the g-file. By this, White's pawns are wrecked. Even though Black does not at once reap any further material compensation, White's scattered pawns are very hard to defend.

23 gxh ♘f5

Now this is possible after White's error on move 20.

24 ♔f2

White does not even try to defend his weak d4 pawn. If 24 ♖ad1? ♘e3 or 24 ♖fd1 ♖g8+ 25 ♔f2 ♖g4 followed by a harvest along the fourth rank.

24 ... ♘cxd4
25 ♗xd4 ♘xd4
26 c4

A most miserable and depressing position to defend, the more so for Nigel, who after an impressive first cycle in Brussels had collapsed in the second, beating only Portisch, but losing to Hübner, Nunn and Kasparov. 26 ♗d3 could be

tried. Short's move allows Korchnoi to deflect White's c-pawn by force to b5. Thus Black can create two connected passed pawns in the d and e-files.

26 ... ♘b3
27 ♖ad1 ♘c5
28 ♗b5 ♗xb5
29 cxb5 ♔g6
30 ♖g1+ ♔f5
31 ♔e3 ♖c8
32 ♖g7

If 32 ♖c1 d4+!

32 ... ♘b3
33 ♖d3 d4+

The passed pawns commence their inexorable advance; ... e5 can follow if required, but it is not needed.

34 ♔f3 ♖c3!
35 ♖xc3 dxc3
36 ♖c7 c2!

The final track: 37 ♖xc2 ♘d4+.

White resigns. The completion of a glorious second cycle for Korchnoi, but a correspondingly unfortunate one for Nigel.

— The Players TV commentaries

1	e4	e6
2	d4	d5
3	♘c3	♗b4
4	e5	c5
5	a3	♗xc3+
6	bxc3	♘e7
7	♘f3	♛a5
8	♗d2	♘bc6

SHORT: I have to admit that I'm really disgusted with my play so far in this tournament, especially in the last three games. I'm just totally fed up with the proceedings. I'd be quite happy just to agree a draw here and go home. Well, there's one move I'd like to play here, and that's h4, but to be honest I haven't the energy to push my pawn that far.

9	♗e2	cxd4
10	cxd4	♛a4

SHORT: I could continue as in Sokolov-Yusupov with 11 ♗e3. Actually I've been thinking of playing this line myself as Black and I was slightly afriad of ♗e3, so I'll give it a whirl.

11	♗e3

KORCHNOI: So what do I have here? I have the idea ♘f5, to take on e3, but he castles, I take on e3, he takes and presumably I have to castle, then he plays ♘g5 or ♘g5 and has a strong attacking position. I need an ending in this position. Well the ending, according to theoretical discoveries, is much better for White, but I'm not afraid of anybody in this type of ending. I have great experience in the French.

11	...	b6
12	♛d3	♘b4
13	♛b5+	♛xb5
14	♗xb5+	♘bc6

SHORT: My biggest problem here is my weak squares on the queenside, but I've already analysed this position, or at least looked at it. I want to re-route my dark-squared bishop and prevent him gaining counterplay with ♘a5 and ♘c4.

15	♗d2

KORCHNOI: Yes this is logical and very scientific. I think the first game was played about 30 years ago by Smyslov. He puts his bishop to c3, king to d2 and proceeded with an attack on the queenside. So, I develop myself. ♗d7 threatens ♘xe5.

15	...	♗d7
16	♗a6	f6

SHORT: It seems like I've had another attack of brain death. I remember now looking at this position with John Nunn and I have just completely forgotten what my conclusion was. I remember one of John's comments; he said that Viktor would play f6 for certain here. Either I take or I leave this pawn, but if I leave it, then it could get uncomfortable. Maybe he gets some pressure down the f-file. So I'll simplify and open the game up a little bit for my bishops.

17 exf6 gxf6
18 ♗c3

KORCHNOI: He wants to play ♘h4. I may play ♘f5 immediately, preventing ♘h4, and perhaps this is the best move. Again, he has two bishops and I have a lot of weaknesses around. Should I play for a draw, for equality, or for a win? If for equality, I have to keep my pawns on their places. Well, I have enough weaknesses already, but I believe in my star and I believe that I may outplay him.

18 ... h5

SHORT: My God, what on earth is that. It looks like a pretty ridiculous move to me. I'm not quite sure what he's trying to do. I mean, this gives me a tempo to block-

ade. I expected simply ♘f5 and ♘d6 coming to e4. This move looks somehow absurd. Anyway, I've decided to give up thinking today, so I'll just play ♘h4 to prevent ♘g6 or ♘f5.

19 ♘h4

KORCHNOI: Logical. Yes, he wants to proceed with his attack against the black central pawns. He wants to play f4, f5. Okay, when he plays f4, I play f5 myself, and put my knight to e4. Okay, my next move is obvious.

19 ... ♚f7

SHORT: I suppose he's trying to gain some counterplay with ♖ag8 and ♖g4, but big deal! It's not so terrifying. I can always play g3, so I'll simply castle. He can play e5, but this is very risky: I simply take and play ♖ae1. Actually I think he has mishandled this slightly.

20 0-0 ♖ag8
21 f4

KORCHNOI: Well, he presumably also believes in his star and thinks that he may just crush me. Well, I have my own plan. I'm going to sacrifice something.

21 ... ♖g4

SHORT: I've got a sneaking suspicion he's going to take my knight on h4, but this doesn't look especially worrying. After 22 g3 ♖xh4 23 gxh4 ♘f5, it's very risky.

It's a bit of a gamble for him to give away an exchange like this. My rooks may suddenly become very good.

22 g3   ♖xh4
23 gxh4   ♘f5

SHORT: I think I have a very strong reply now. Simply ♔f2. If he takes my h-pawn, it is much too slow. He has to take my d-pawn and then I get rid of this lousy bishop on c3. He has only one pawn for his exchange, and I can play c4 and open up the game.

24 ♔f2

KORCHNOI: Very good move. Otherwise I could play ♖g8+ and ♖g4. Well, I have to recapture something. I need some compensation for the exchange.

24 ...   ♘cxd4
25 ♗xd4   ♘xd4

SHORT: Well, I could play ♗d3 to prevent this knight going back to f5, but then he has some chances with ♖c8 or e5, even ♗b5, who knows? But 26 c4 looks very strong here. The moment I get my rooks into the game, it becomes very uncomfortable for him.

26 c4

KORCHNOI: Oh, this is a mistake. Instead he had to play ♖d1 or ♗d3, and the position was about equal. But this is an obvious mistake. He overlooks my manoeuvre.

26 ...   ♘b3

SHORT: I completely forgot about that. Very strange, my pawn has been defending b3 and I just moved it away. I just completely missed this idea. My rook's attacked; I move it and his knight comes to c5, then my bishop is really embarrassed on a6. So if I play 27 ♖ad1 ♘c5 28 ♗b5 ♗xb5 29 cxb5 ♘e4+ 30 ♔e3 ♘d6, he brings his knight to f5 and wins my h-pawn. Well, he can get two pawns, but my rooks are becoming very active. Possibly my best is to take on d5 and just give up the exchange. Then I'm just worse and only he has chances to win. Okay, let's move my rook.

27 ♖ad1

KORCHNOI: Also very optimistic. He could simply take 27 cxd5, when I take 27 ... ♘xa1 28 dxe6+ ♗xe6 29 ♖xa1, Black stands better. But it was still about equal game. Well now my move is obvious.

27 ...   ♘c5
28 ♗b5   ♗xb5
29 cxb5

KORCHNOI: And my next move, well, he has not overlooked but obviously underestimated. King g6. I'm going to push all my pawns together with the king and all my pieces in coordination.

271

29 ...   &g6

SHORT: Oh dear, it shows what pathetic form I'm in at the moment. I didn't even consider this move. Of course it's very strong simply putting the king on f5. My rooks are completely out of the game. I guess the position is even losing now. That's incredible, he just has this great wall of pawns. I can't attack anything here. Anyway I'll try to activate my rook.

30   &g1+   &f5
31   &e3

KORCHNOI: Black is obviously better, but should I defend my 7th rank. I need to do something quickly because there is a threat in the position. If he plays &g7, then &dg1, then &f7, then &g5 mate. Somehow I have to chase his king from the third rank. I believe the move &c8 will serve this purpose.

31	...	&c8
32	&g7	&b3
33	&d3	d4+
34	&f3	&c3
35	&xc3	dc
36	&c7	c2

SHORT: I didn't even see this crazy move c2. Well, if I take, &d4+, so obviously I have to resign. It just shows what bad form I'm in. Almost any beginner can see this.

  0:1

GAME TWENTY-NINE
PORTISCH-KASPAROV

1 c4 e6 2 ♘c3 d5 3 d4 ♗e7 4 ♘f3 ♘f6 5 ♗g5
h6 6 ♗h4 0-0 7 e3 b6 8 ♖c1 ♗b7 9 ♗d3
dxc4 10 ♗xc4 ♘bd7 11 0-0 c5 12 ♕e2 a6
13 a4 cxd4 14 exd4 ♘h5 15 ♗xe7 ♕xe7
16 d5 ♘f4 17 ♕e3 ♕f6 18 ♘e4 ♕f5 19 ♘g3
♕f6 20 ♘e4 ♕f5 21 ♘g3 ♕f6 ½:½

GAME TWENTY-NINE

PORTISCH - KASPAROV

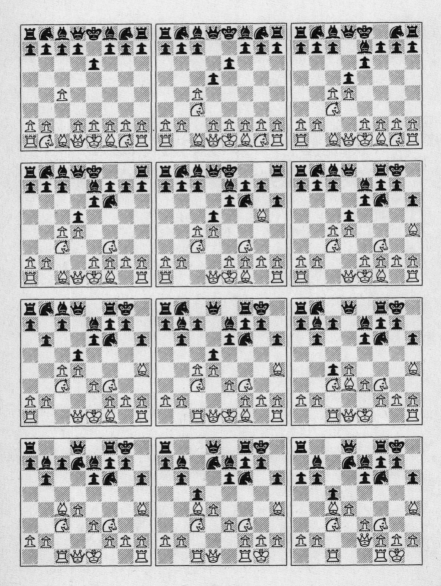

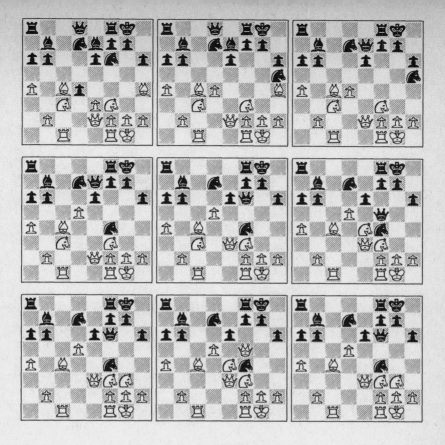

1/2:1/2

Portisch - Kasparov

This is the last round. Kasparov had already won the tournament by a possibly record margin for this kind of event, and he did not need to push for a win with the Black pieces. Portisch actually said "thank you", when Kasparov offered the draw. Kasparov, in relaxed and endearing fashion, even found time to sign autographs for admirers during the game!

1	c4	e6
2	♘c3	d5
3	d4	♗e7
4	♘f3	♘f6
5	♗g5	h6
6	♗h4	

After the battering he received in the preceding rounds Portisch could scarcely have been expected to enter a sever theoretical dispute after 6 ♗xf6.

6	...	0-0
7	e3	b6

The trusty Tartakower-Makogonov-Bondarevsky system.

8	♖c1	♗b7
9	♗d3	dxc4
10	♗xc4	♘bd7
11	0-0	c5
12	♕e2	

12 dxc5 ♘xc5 13 ♕e2 a6

14 ♖fd1 ♕e8 15 ♘e5 b5 16 ♘xb5 (Kasparov-Karpov -36-World Championship Moscow 1984/85) appears doubtful after 16 ... ♕b8!! Of course, under present circumstances Portisch is not going to enter that kind of snake-pit.

12	...	a6!
13	a4	cxd4

13 ... ♘e4 14 ♘xe4 ♗xe4 15 ♗g3 was tried in Kortschnoi-Karpov, (3) Menas 1981. It also led to a draw, but the text is more efficient.

14	exd4	♘h5
15	♗xe7	♕xe7
16	d5	♘f4
17	♕e3	♕f6
18	♘e4	♕f5

19	♘g3	

Not 19 ♘d6? ♕g4!

19	...	♕f6

20 ♘e4   ♕f5

Kasparov-Karpov (34) Moscow 1984/85 ended here as ½:½. Portisch plays one more move.

21 ♘g3   ♕f6

Drawn.

The fifth round game between Korchnoi and Short.

GAME THIRTY
NUNN-HÜBNER

1 e4 e6 2 d4 d5 3 ♘c3 ♗b4 4 e5 ♕d7 5 ♗d2
b6 6 ♗b5 c6 7 ♗a4 a5 8 a3 ♗f8 9 ♘ce2 ♗a6
10 c3 ♘e7 11 ♘f3 ♘f5 12 0-0 ♗e7 13 ♖e1
♗xe2 14 ♕xe2 ♘a6 15 ♗c2 ♘c7 16 a4 g6
17 ♖ad1 h5 18 g3 ♔f8 19 ♔g2 ♔g7 20 h3
♖ag8 21 ♖h1 ♕d8 22 b4 ♕a8 23 g4 ♘h6
24 ♘g5 b5 25 bxa5 ♕xa5 26 axb5 ♘xb5
27 c4 ♘xd4 28 ♘xe6+ ♘xe6 29 ♗xa5
♘f4+ 30 ♔f3 ♘xe2 31 ♔xe2 hxg4 32 hxg4
½:½

GAME THIRTY
NUNN - HÜBNER

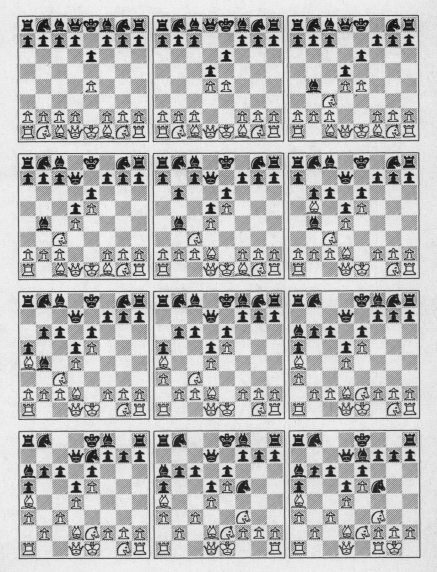

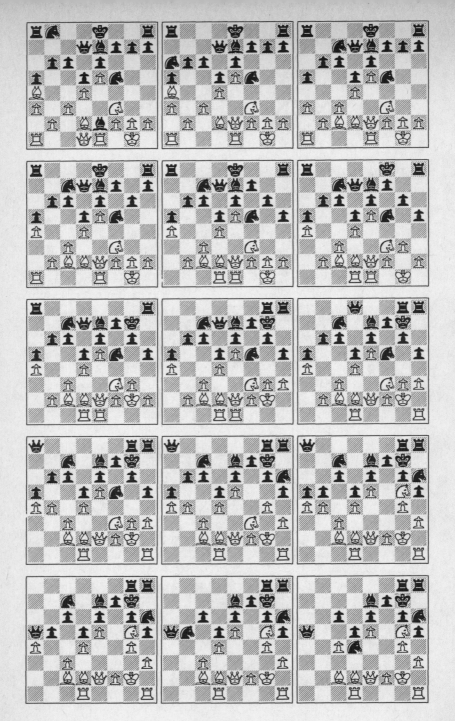

1/2:1/2

Nunn - Hübner

1	e4	e6
2	d4	d5
3	♘c3	

The French was popular at OHRA, perhaps because 3 ♘d2 (boring but + =) is going gradually out of fashion now that Karpov is no longer setting trends as World Champion.

3	...	♗b4
4	e5	♕d7

Petrosian used to favour this very slow treatment, without, or delaying ... c5, but I have never really trusted it.

Vaganian suffered a complete disaster v Chandler on the Black side in the celebrated England-USSR match in Dubai, a few weeks earlier. Nunn was there, Hübner not.

5	♗d2	b6
6	♗b5!	

This I like very much. It seems strange to send White's KB into the desert wilderness of the Queen's wing, where only a hostile phalanx of Black pawns awaits it. However, the point is to relocate White's KB along the lush pastures of the b1-h7 diagonal. Meanwhile, White tempts weaknesses amongst the Black pawns and makes it more difficult for Black to play ... ♘c6.

6	...	c6
7	♗a4	a5
8	a3	

Now White, has, if necessary, a haven for his KB on a2.

8	...	♗f8
9	♘ce2	

Vital preparation for c3, cementing White's pawn chain.

9	...	♗a6

The Black QB seems influential along the a6-f1 diagonal, but in reality it is beating into empty space, as Black's 13th move will admit. White's coming manoeuvre with his KB is substantially more significant.

10	c3	♘e7
11	♘f3	♘f5

Not a permanent outpost.

In due course White's g4 will knock out the props from this Knight.

12 0-0 &e7
13 ♖e1 &xe2

A major decision. White now has the Bishop pair, plus the chance to break open the position on both flanks. Otherwise, however, White will play ♘f4 and Black's QB will be optically but not actually active. Also, in his cramped state Black needs a6 for his QN.

14 ♕xe2 ♘a6
15 &c2 ♘c7
16 a4 g6

The resourceful Hübner carries out all the sensible defensive consolidation work that is possible. Ultimately, however, his position is sterile. It is up to Nunn when and how he tries to blast through Black's barricades.

17 ♖ad1 h5
18 g3 ♔f8

Black's King is also not safe on the other side of the board, where White can play b4. Hübner decides to plant his King on g7, but to mass defensive units all around it.

19 ♔g2

Methodical preparation for g4.

19 ... ♔g7
20 h3 ♖ag8
21 ♖h1 ♕d8

22 b4 ♕a8

At this point Nunn decides the time is ripe for tactical demolition of the Black fortress.

But Nunn is wrong. If he was to continue squashing any Black activity (eg ♖a1, stopping ... b5) Black is strategically lost in my view, and in the long run quite helpless against a well-timed g4 by White.

23 g4? ♘h6
24 ♘g5 b5!

Even now White could try ♖a1, but he has already permitted Black to create targets on the Q-side. Nunn launches a combination, but it doesn't win.

25 bxa5 ♕xa5!
26 axb5 ♘xb5
27 c4 ♘xd4!

The tactical justification of Black's play — counter-attacking White's Queen.

28 ♘xe6 +

A bombshell, planning to meet 28 ... fxe6 with 29 ♕d3 attacking a5 and g6.

28 ...   ♘xe6!!

Hübner also has his tricks. This is hard to visualise in advance, since Black relieves his attack against the White Queen from d4 ...

29 ♗xa5

Only to renew it from f4 ...

29 ...   ♘f4 +
30 ♔f3   ♘xe2
31 ♔xe2   hxg4
32 hxg4

Drawn. Eg. 32 ... ♖a8 (planning ... ♖a2) 33 ♖a1 ♘xg4 34 ♖xh8 ♖xh8 (♔xh8 35 cxd5 cxd5 36 ♗b3 ♘xe5? 37 ♗c3) 35 cxd5 cxd5 36 ♗b3 ♘xe5 37 ♗c3 ♗f6 38 ♗xe5 ♗xe5 39 ♖a5 ♖e8 40 ♖xd5 =.

OFF THE BOARD

The closing ceremony on the evening of 23rd December took place without Robert Hübner, who had left early to avoid an industrial dispute on the French railways ... somewhat to the chagrin of the Brussels organisers who could not see his journey back to Cologne taking him particularly close to France.

But, of the five grandmasters present at the ceremony, the focus of attention was on two only. Gary Kasparov — playing his first tournament for three years, during which time he had been engaged in successive matches against Anatoly Karpov — had won, and won with something to spare, over five top grandmasters.

The verdict on Nigel Short, regarded by many as Kasparov's next serious challenger for the world title, was far from unanimous. After an impressive first five rounds, his results had tailed off.

In fact, after next putting up a respectable performance in a televised quick-play match against Kasparov, Short was to storm to victory in a very strong Icelandic tournament in February. Korchnoi, Ljubojević and Tal were there among his victims.

But the young Englishman already acknowledge that, like Bobby Fischer many years before, he would find the path to Kasparov's crown barred by a phalanx of Soviet grandmasters. There was no certainty that superior talent alone was enough to succeed.

BRUSSELS - OHRA 1986

	Kas	Kor	Hüb	Nun	Sho	Por	
1. G. Kasparov	x x	½ ½	1 1	1 1	0 1	1 ½	$7\frac{1}{2}$
2. V. Korchnoi	½ ½	x x	1 0	½ ½	½ 1	0 1	$5\frac{1}{2}$
3. =R. Hübner	0 0	0 1	x x	1 ½	0 1	½ 1	5
3. =J. Nunn	0 0	½ ½	0 ½	x x	1 1	½ 1	5
5. N. Short	1 0	½ 0	1 0	0 0	x x	½ 1	4
6. L. Portisch	0 ½	1 0	½ 0	½ 0	½ 0	x x	3